SpringerBriefs in Computer Science

For further volumes:
http://www.springer.com/series/10028

Christopher Hofman · Simeon Keates

Countering Brandjacking in the Digital Age

… and Other Hidden Risks to Your Brand

Springer

Christopher Hofman
European Domain Centre
Frederiksberg C
Denmark

Simeon Keates
University of Greenwich
School of Engineering
Kent, UK

ISSN 2191-5768 ISSN 2191-5776 (electronic)
ISBN 978-1-4471-5579-9 ISBN 978-1-4471-5580-5 (eBook)
DOI 10.1007/978-1-4471-5580-5
Springer London Heidelberg New York Dordrecht

Library of Congress Control Number: 2013949721

Printed on acid-free paper

Springer is part of Springer Science+Business Media (www.springer.com)

To my lovely girlfriend Chris and my long-time friend and business partner Nikolaj for support and encouragement

– Christopher Hofman

For my son, Lucian

– Simeon Keates

Contents

Chapter 1
An Introduction to Brand Risk

Abstract In this introductory chapter, we explore the nature of brand risks and discuss the motivation behind the writing of this book. The rise of the internet and social media offer great opportunities for brand owners to increase business and brand recognition. However, they also offer opportunities for less scrupulous people to take advantage of those brands whether for personal gain, illicit purposes or simply out of malice. Brand owners need to be aware of such risks and of the need to develop strategies for identifying and managing them. This chapter provides examples where companies and celebrities have been targeted by cybersquatters. It further then provides a set of definitions through which an understanding of the risks can be developed. Finally, this chapter details the process by which a brand owner can develop a brand risk management process to protect a brand's reputation and value. The development of that process is then explored in the rest of the book.

Keywords Brand • Risk • Design • Internet • Domain names • Cybersquatting • Lawsuits • Definitions • Social media

In 2003, Christopher Hofman started a domain registration service, European Domain Centre (EDC), aimed at helping international companies register domain names in any country worldwide. At that time, it was still common practice to order domain names on the telephone, but EDC created a website, where clients could register any of the 300+ top-level domains. These include global domains such as *.com*, *.org* and country domains such as *co.uk*, *.jp* and *.dk*. This type of service allows companies to protect their brand names easily for any top-level domain in the countries where they are present by defensively acquiring any domain name that they might later wish to use.

However, many of these brand owners discovered that their domain names had already been registered by third parties. Sometimes this was the result of coincidence, for example where names of companies were similar or where the domain being sought was quite generic. For example, *pitchers.com* could be about baseball players or glass jugs. Similarly *bowlers.com* could be about cricket players or hats.

C. Hofman and S. Keates, *Countering Brandjacking in the Digital Age*, SpringerBriefs in Computer Science, DOI: 10.1007/978-1-4471-5580-5_1,

Sometimes, though, the domains had been pre-emptively registered by third parties with the express objective of obtaining financial reward. This was the rise of the infamous cybersquatters, people who purchased domain names predatorily with a view to effectively holding them to ransom. Should a company fail to meet the financial demands of the cybersquatter, then the domain name was often sold to competitors or used to host unwelcome material, either critical of the company or advertising wholly inappropriate material, such as gambling and pornographic sites. Many companies viewed cybersquatters as little more than online blackmailers. Unfortunately, though, recovering a domain name from a cybersquatter was a long, arduous and often very expensive process. A number of companies took the pragmatic decision that it was often cheaper in the long run to simply meet the cybersquatters' demands. Even when the brand owners did know that they had to hurry to secure their domain names in a timely manner, they usually reacted very late, in some cases too late. It would later cost them immense effort, time and resources to recover their domain names.

Celebrities have also fallen victim to cybersquatters, with Madonna fighting a public battle to reclaim *madonna.com* in 2000 [5] and Jennifer Lopez taking similar action in 2009 over *jenniferlopez.org* and *jenniferlopez.net*, both held by an alleged cybersquatter [6]. Both were victorious in their action. However, Sting fared less well in his attempts to secure the rights to *sting.com*, with the World Intellectual Property Organization (WIPO) deciding that "sting" was a generic term and therefore could not be assigned exclusively to him [5]. If he had registered the site before the domain had been taken by a third party, he would not have been in the position of having to contest its ownership through WIPO. As with many things in life, pre-emptive defensive actions can prevent large legal bills and avoid unpleasant circumstances.

With the prominence of these high-profile cases, most companies are now aware of the risks of simple domain name cybersquatting, although that does not mean that they necessarily have developed strategies to deal with the issue. However, a new trend in the use of technology over recent years has led to the problem for companies increasing substantially.

A company's web presence is no longer restricted to its own web site. Many companies now have, for example, Twitter and Facebook logos on their home pages. The rise of social media has changed how users, and thus customers, find information and post opinions on the web. The business model behind most companies' social media presence is that networks of friends and contacts will usually share information about their likes and dislikes. Getting their company name or brands into those networks, typically through a person opting to "like" or "follow" it, gives the company a presence in the collective conscience of the network. In effect, getting their company into a network of friends is a very efficient advertising mechanism. Rather than identifying a collection of people at whom they wish to target their advertising, they simply need to identify one or two key people and the networks those people have established will automatically raise awareness of the company and its products through the constructs already in place through sites such as Facebook.

However while social media offers companies new and innovative ways to communicate with their customers, the increase in potential points of contact with customers also offers opportunities for the latest incarnation of cybersquatters. Each new social media technology or site offers yet another opportunity for cybersquatting. Even the largest companies can occasionally get caught out by the cybersquatters. So what hope is there for smaller companies, who are often just managing to keep their web sites active and free from hacking attacks?

It is easy to observe history repeating itself. This time the same companies that missed out on registering their domain names are now missing out on their rightful social media usernames, such as *facebook.com/cocacola* or *twitter.com/prada*. This raises a fundamental question—why are companies often so slow to react to the new opportunities and threats in cyberspace? Why do they not take more rigorous action to protect their brand identity on the Internet? Should brand owners take this seriously, or is it considered "desirable" rather than "essential" to their business?

Markmonitor, a corporate domain registrar that compiles a very informative brandjacking index, found that the top 10 global media brands lost out on an incredible 53 billion visits annually via trademark infringing domain names [4]. There were 43 unique sites selling counterfeit products waiting to trap users who mistyped the domain names of those top 10 brands in a web browser.

The Internet is evolving constantly, and social media is just the latest buzz. Surpassing Google in 2010 as the most visited website, US internet users already spend 36 % of their online time at Facebook [7]. Brands want to be where their customers are. If that is on social media, then brands will have to communicate to them via this channel. What is needed is a designed solution to protect brands from the threats lurking in this new cyberspace.

1.1 Designing a Solution

If even multinational giants, with their abundance or resources, can get caught out by the latest cybersquatting tactics, then it is clearly unrealistic to expect much smaller companies to be able to identify and manage the risk on their own. Instead, it is much more useful to consider the following question:

How can companies manage brand risk on the Internet?

In this book, we will consider approaches to answering this question and exemplify those approaches through the design of a "brandjacking awareness" model. We will begin by examining the concepts of "brand" and the overall landscape of "brand risk" on the Internet. These concepts are then examined through case studies of six European companies. These companies include a small vendor, a medium-sized enterprise and a national company. The data collected from these case studies are then used to inform the design of an example prototype for helping companies identify and address cybersquatting brand risks on the Internet.

1.2 Definitions

It is worth beginning by defining the concepts of "brand" and "brand risk."

Brand: A brand is an intangible asset comprising of all publicly identifiable knowledge associated with a particular product, service or company.

Brand risk: According to Clifton and Maughan:

Brand risk accommodates all the risks and uncertainties about the sustainability of profitable demand for the brand, together with its continued capacity to create value, influence or commitment amongst each of its key constituencies—not just customers [3].

Brand risk is not only reputation risk. David Abrahams, a brand risk consultant, states that a *"brand is not a reputation. It follows that reputation risk is an incomplete concept of brand risk"* [1].

It is also worth examining the nature of the brand risks, effectively what forms brand risks can take in the online world. We will examine these later in this book. However, for brevity we will classify all such threats under the description "malicious sites." This description is intended to include sites that are designed to steal business from the brand owner, to tarnish the brand owner's reputation, to promote a rival's product or simply to trade on the back of the brand owner's reputation. An example of this latter point would be the use of click-through advertisement revenue, when an owner of a malicious site may fill the web page with paid advertisement links.

Malicious sites are a subset of a wider classification of "threat sites." In addition to malicious sites, these also include sites that are fully legitimate, but may cause confusion and brand risks through coincidence or proximity of products and names rather than out of malicious intent.

It is also necessary to define the types of solutions that we will discuss in this book.

Brand Risk Management Models: The models are more abstract representations that represent generic solutions. They can be modified and applied to specific brand owner needs to develop the Brand Risk Management Strategy,

Brand Risk Management Strategy: The strategy is the high-level description of brand risk management, defined in terms of aims, for a specific brand owner. This is the executive summary description of how a brand owner defines what is needed in terms of managing brand risk. It does not include reference to operational or tactical issues, but is more a series of statements of intent.

Brand Risk Management Process: The process is the operationalization of the strategy, effectively a summary list of activities and tasks describing who does what, when and how.

Brand Risk Management Tools: The tools are the products or systems that facilitate the completion of the tasks and activities that constitute the Brand Risk Management Process. These can include, for example, visualisation and project management software.

Brand Risk Management System: The system is the combined range of all Brand Risk Management activities and includes the Strategy, the process and the tools. It is the comprehensive Brand Risk Management activity for a brand owner.

1.3 The Role of Design

Whenever designing a new model or system, it is helpful to adopt a proven design methodology. One of the most flexible such approaches is that of the Design Research Methodology (DRM). Applying the DRM supports both the design of a prototype, but also consideration of the process of design itself [2].

The DRM consists of 4 stages:

- Stage 1: Criteria—establishing the measures of success.
- Stage 2: Descriptive study I—understanding and explaining the problem to be solved.
- Stage 3: Prescriptive study—developing a solution.
- Stage 4: Descriptive study II—evaluating the solution and describing possible revisions.

Looking at each of these stages in turn:

1.3.1 Stage 1-Criteria

The first activity in any design approach is to understand and establish the measures of success. In other words, we need to clearly explain what a brand owner would like its brand risk management system to achieve. For our purposes here, the headline measures of success are straightforward to identify. An effective brand risk management system is clearly one that successfully controls and manages all brand risks.

If we dig down a little deeper, that control can either mean avoidance of a threat through pre-emptive actions or rapid and effective responses to emergent threats. In the case of brandjacking threats, a successful pre-emptive strategy would include the systematic registration of all potential cybersquatting sites.

However, even the most comprehensive preventative strategy cannot militate against all possible threats—there is always the possibility of "unknown unknowns" to paraphrase former United States Secretary of Defense, Donald Rumsfeld. Where such threats begin to emerge, it is imperative that a brand owner recognises the threat as quickly as possible and then formulates an equally swift and effective range of countermeasures. The old adage of "a stitch in time saves nine" is very much applicable here. The longer a brand risk remains unchallenged, the more severe the potential damage to the brand will be.

Finally, should all the control measures fail to mitigate the threat, a media management strategy is required to acknowledge failings and reassure the public that the brand owner will be learning the relevant lessons and taking appropriate steps to address the underlying issues.

To summarise, an effective brand risk management system should be based on three principal steps:

- Step 1: Pre-emptive action—identify the probable sources of brand risks and move to neutralise those risks.
- Step 2: Early detection and rapid response—employ an active monitoring culture and have clear plans of action developed and in place for swift deployment.
- Step 3: Media management—where the control measures cannot bring the threat under control, then acknowledge the issue openly and implement the measures necessary to ensure a repeat is not possible.

The steps can be arrived at with a little common sense and thinking around the problem. They are high-level and quite generic. The devil, as the saying goes, is in the detail. Stage 2 of the DRM focuses on obtaining a better understanding of the details of the problem so potential solutions can then be developed.

1.3.2 Stage 2-Descriptive Study I

Before a solution, in this case a brand risk management system, can be developed, it is necessary to understand and be able to explain the problem to be solved.

At a high level, though, the basic questions to be addressed can be summarised as follows:

- What is a potential risk?
- What is an active risk?
- How does a brand owner identify types of risk?
- How does a brand owner identify potential sources of risk?
- How does a brand owner know which risks to monitor?
- How does a brand owner know which risks to act upon and/or prioritise?
- Once a risk has been identified, what is the best strategy for addressing it?
- What lessons can be learned from each risk?

Chapters 2 and 3 focus on answering these questions. With that enhanced understanding, the next Stage of the DRM looks at the development of a potential solution.

1.3.3 Stage 3-Developing a Solution

The basic theory behind managing brand risk is known. However, many companies still struggle to implement effective brand management strategies. There are several reasons for this:

- A failure to understand the nature of the risk.
- A failure to clearly allocate responsibility.
- A failure to develop a sufficient robust solution, at least in part because of the preceding points.

Central to developing an effective strategy to managing brand risk is the need for clear information about the nature of the risk. As with all risks, the information that really matters is:

- The proximity of the risk—Is it an active risk? Is it a potential risk? In what timescale might it move from a potential risk to an active (live) one?
- The severity of the risk—Is it a risk that threatens the survival of the brand? Or is it a risk that will cause limited damage?
- The trending of the risk—Is the threat of the risk increasing or diminishing? How rapidly is the threat changing?
- The control measures for the risk—What control measures are available and which one(s) will be the most effective?

Traditional models for managing brand risk focus on primarily written processes. These processes can be very complex. In this book, we will look at employing the techniques of visualisation and interaction design to examine whether more innovative solutions can be developed. Chapter 4 explores an approach for how brand owners can go about developing their own brand risk management processes.

1.3.4 Stage 4-Descriptive Study II

The final stage of the DRM is to reflect on the effectiveness of the solution that has been developed, or in this case could be developed. Chapter 5 discusses what can be learned from examining brand risk management processes and how companies should respond to the challenges that they face in the digital age.

References

1. Abrahams, D.: Brand risk—adding risk literacy to brand management. Gower Publishing, United Kingdom (2008)
2. Blessing, L., Chakrabarti, A.: DRM: A design research methodology. Springer-Verlag, London (2009)
3. Clifton, R., Maughan, E.: The future of brands: Twenty-five visions. Inter-brand and Macmillan, London (2000)
4. Markmonitor: Brandjacking index—Luxury goods. https://www.markmonitor.com/download/bji/BrandjackingIndex-SpecialEdition2010-LuxuryGoods.pdf (2010)
5. Reuters: Madonna wins domain name battle. http://archives.cnn.com/2000/TECH/computing/10/16/madonna.cybersquatter.reut/ (2000). 16 Oct 2000
6. Reuters: Jennifer Lopez wins cybersquatting case. http://www.pcmag.com/article2/0,2817,2344801,00.asp (2009). 9 Apr 2009
7. Swartz, J: Time spent on Facebook, Twitter, YouTube grows. USA Today. http://usatoday30.usatoday.com/tech/news/2010-08-02-networking02_ST_N.htm (2010). 1 Aug 2010

Chapter 2
An Overview of Branding and its Associated Risks

Abstract This chapter examines what a brand is and how much a brand is worth for a company. A definition of what makes a brand is provided, along with examples of how brand value can be increased. The value of brands has increased substantially with the rise of mass media and globalisation. While this has clearly been of benefit to brand owners, who have seen a consequent rise in the value of their brands, it simultaneously makes those brands more attractive for exploitation by others. Brand risks can come in many different types and this chapter presents 15 such types of risk. It provides examples of how these risks can arise and provides quantitative estimates of the adverse impacts that can result from such risks.

Keywords Brand • Trademark • Domain name • Brand risk • Brand value • Types of risk • Internet • Social media • Search engine

2.1 What is a Brand?

The notion of brands originated in the nineteenth century, when production moved from local communities to centralized factories. Factories would literally burn ("brand") their logo on barrels before shipping them to customers. It became a way to compete with local, well known products and the "brand" increased general familiarity with products from distant factories.

As the use of branding became more widespread, it became necessary to regulate their use. The first trademarks were registered around 1870. The registering of a trademark is effectively the legal birth date of a brand. However, a trademark will only be registered as intellectual property if it is defined as unique within a geographic territory. While trademarks are usually text based, it is possible to register a symbol, a graphical design, a colour, a sound or even a unique smell.

C. Hofman and S. Keates, *Countering Brandjacking in the Digital Age*,
SpringerBriefs in Computer Science, DOI: 10.1007/978-1-4471-5580-5_2,

From around 1900, commercialization with slogans and merchandise started. When mass media such as radio and TV caught on, manufacturers were able to reach the masses efficiently and could develop relationships with their customers more easily. The notion of the "brand" was central in this strategy. It was an effective shorthand description of a narrative. In advertising, to quote the old adage, time is money. An effective brand allows the seller an advertising shortcut as long as the brand has a clearly identified "meaning," ideally a set of attributes that a potential consumer identifies with and finds appealing.

Over the years branding has gained increasing importance, and is today an extremely important part of most customer purchase decisions. A brand can be summed up by the following quote:

> A brand is a set of mental associations, held by the consumer, which add to the perceived value of a product or service [32].

Brand components include, but are not limited to [34]:

- trademarks
- domain names
- sub-brands
- product packaging
- manufacturer and trade names
- advertising of the product
- distribution
- celebrity endorsements
- shelf displays at retailers.

2.2 What is Brand Value?

Brand value is the estimated value of the brand as part of the total estimated company value. In 1978, brand value was largely ignored. In a study from that year only 5 % of the market value of companies on the Dow Jones index were intangibles, which included the value of the brand. By 2007, this proportion had risen to a staggering potential 72 % of the total company value [34]. A similar study from [39] showed that tangible assets accounted only for 30–40 % of a business's value. In that study, the major portion of intangible assets were attributed to the value of the brand.

Companies such as Interbrand calculate the brand value of the top 100 brands annually and the Coca Cola brand tops their list with an estimated value of US$78 billion [30]. Brand value is particularly relevant when it comes to calculating the sales price of a company. Gillette's brand value was estimated at US$18 billion [29] in 2005, which is 32 % of the US$57 billion price that Procter & Gamble paid for the whole company the same year [6].

The calculation of a brand's value is obviously quite complicated and involves a range of possible variables to be considered. Interbrand looks at ten components in a company. Each component is given an attributable factor, which when summed up gives the total brand value. The brand protection component, i.e. the ability to protect intellectual property, is estimated to be 5 % of the total value of a brand. The other components are more directed towards the market, such as positioning and marketing, but they are all exposed to brand risk factors such as authenticity, consistency, presence in customer mind and relevance.

2.3 Brand Risk

If there is no "brand value," then there is inherently no "brand risk." Brand risk is used to describe any element that can damage the brand, and consequently diminish the total brand value [15]. Brand risk has existed since the birth of brands. Sometimes the risk arises from crudely malicious claims, such as alleging that a factory's products contain ingredients that are harmful or dangerous. Fast food chains, such as MacDonald's and KFC, have been the victims of such claims in the past [13].

Sometimes, though, the damage is self-inflicted, such as in the infamous cases of the 1985 Austrian wine antifreeze scandal [51] and Gerald Ratner's disparaging comments in 1991 about one of the products sold in the chain of jewellery shops that bore his name [17]. Both scandals caused devastating damage that took years of rebranding efforts to overcome, with Ratner's becoming Signet Group and the Austrian wine industry widely considered to have taken 10 years to recover from the antifreeze incident. Gerald Ratner has received the unfortunate accolade in the UK now of being permanently associated with such self-inflicted business faux pas through the expression "doing a Ratner" [17].

Both of these scandals pre-date the rise of the Internet. Nowadays, such rumours could suddenly spread like wildfire due to the ease of distribution, causing even more extensive damage even more quickly.

This brand risk challenge comes at a time when brands are bigger than ever. The Deloitte consultant Jonathan Copulsky's brand paradox mode, shown in Fig. 2.1, indicates that when a brand's value increases, the brand is exposed to ever-increasing brand risk. Big brands are built on closer customer relationships, but these relationships are fragile. With bigger brands come bigger brand risks. Copulsky states *brand risk is a natural consequence of operating decisions that you make* ([15], p. 89). However, no brand can stand still and such operating decisions have to be made on a regular basis in order to compete.

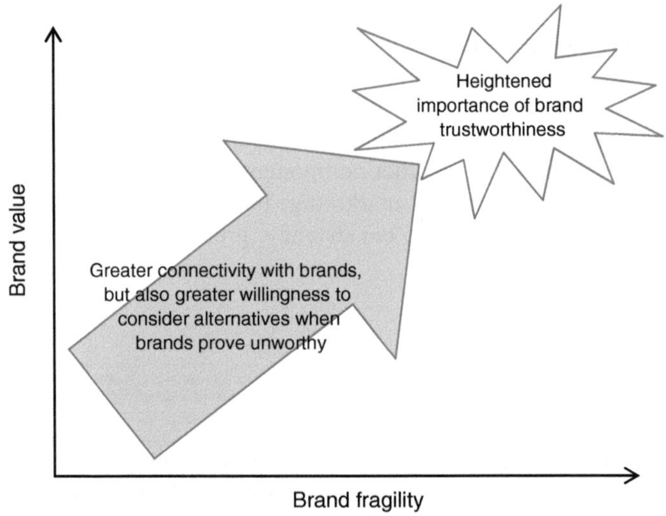

Fig. 2.1 Copulsky's brand paradox model (Copulsky 2011)

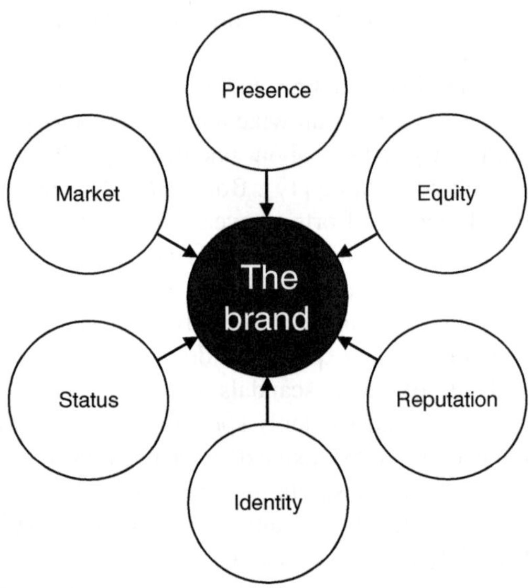

Fig. 2.2 The 6 Components of brand risk (after Abrahams 2008)

2.3.1 Brand Risks on the Internet

Identifying online brand risks is a difficult challenge. The ever-changing technology and users' responses to those changes make for a complex terrain for brand owners to navigate. However, attempts have been made to provide structure to the challenge. For example, David Abrahams has developed a Brand Risk model ([1], p. 21), which maps six components where brand risk can occur—see Fig. 2.2.

The Brand Risk model was developed to address generic sources of brand risks, but was not developed to explicitly address online risks. It is possible to perform such a mapping, though.

Table 2.1 shows such a mapping and illustrates 14 different online brand risks as identified by Brian H. Murray director at Cyveillance, a leading specialist in online security solutions [40]. We have added an additional threat, "social media user names," to the list to bring the list more up to date.

It is worth exploring each of these brand risks in detail and to show the negative effects they can have for a brand's value.

2.3.1.1 Identity Risk

Originally trademarks, logos and trade names were the predominant brand identifiers. On the Internet domain names and social media usernames largely replace them as the principal brand identifiers. Users use them as road signs to be directed to the brand's website or social media site. When a brand does not control all relevant road signs, then users can be diverted to third party content websites instead or reach a dead end. Should the road signs belong to a third party intent on damaging the company's brand then that represents a very significant threat to the brand. The best that a brand owner can hope for is an empty page (the dead end referred to earlier). More likely, the page will contain a list of competitor sites, spurious claims about the brand owner or even a deliberately fraudulent site masquerading as the official site, but intent on stealing business directly from the brand owner. Not only does such a site represent lost business for the brand owner, but also represents a further risk if the products sold are poor quality or if the products never arrive at all. Users may well blame the legitimate brand owners rather than the fraudsters who own the duplicitous site.

Table 2.1 Murray's 14 + 1 online brand risks [40]

Table	Brand risk model component
Cybersquatting	Identity risk
Typosquatting	Identity risk
Social media usernames	Identity risk
Phishing	Presence risk
Links	Presence risk
E-mail	Presence risk
Search engine manipulation	Presence risk
Paid placement	Presence risk
Affiliates	Presence risk
Distributors	Equity risk
Counterfeiting	Equity risk
Grey market	Equity risk
Digital piracy	Equity risk
Rumours	Reputation risk
User complaints	Reputation risk

2.3.1.2 Domain Names

The domain name is the address of the company's website, such as www.cocacola.com. To date, 250 million domain names have been registered and approximately two thirds of these are *.com* domains [20]. The other half of registered domains consists of more than 300 top-level domains. The top-level domains can either be geographically based, such as *.de, .dk, .es, .co.uk* representing Germany, Denmark, Spain and the UK respectively. Alternatively, they may be based on the function of the domain owner, such as *.org* or *.gov* being a non-profit organisation or a government agency respectively. Many users type the website address directly in the browser to access a website. From an early stage of the Internet third party registrants found they could get some of this traffic when users made a spelling mistake or incorrectly guessed the address, such as using *.com* instead of a country-specific domain, such as *.co.uk* or *.dk*. To avoid the possibility of mistyping a site's web address, some users opt for typing the name of the company into a search engine e.g. [23], rather than attempting to type the name straight into the browser. The search engine results typically offer a very brief snapshot of the target page without the user having to go to the page. This offers a basic level of protection in some cases against malicious attempts at redirection.

However, even this approach is not infallible, as the owners of the malicious sites (as defined in Sect. 1.1.1) now regularly disguise the nature of their site by providing enough legitimate content to a search engine to generate an apparently correct, i.e. respectable and trustworthy-looking, return to a search engine. Search engines operate along known behaviour patterns that are easy to reverse engineer and to then provide pseudo-authentic responses to in order to appear authentic.

While some malicious site owners are motivated to simply damage a brand any way they can, the majority of owners of such sites are looking to make a profit from their deception. The simplest way to achieve this is through the use of click-through advertising. Services such as Google AdSense pay a small amount of money to the owners of sites that contain links to a site owned by a paying (legitimate) Google customer. The owners of those legitimate sites often do not know where their visitors are coming from nor do they have any control over payments made to the owners of the malicious sites, as the process is entirely automated. Websites that are designed to profit from such click-through traffic are often called "parked places." They are usually found around simple misspellings of a company's usual home page address. Figure 2.3 shows an example for a simple misspelling of *gnnetcom.com*.

It can be estimated that GN Netcom is missing out on approximately 480 visits per month. We can estimate that traffic as follows.

Estimated number of searches for "GN Netcom"; "gnnetcom";
"gnnetcom.com" from Google Adwords traffic estimator = 1571per day
Estimated number of direct URL entries = 10% ofdaily searches
= c. 157 per day
Estimated mistyping+ misspelling rate = 10% of daily searches
= 16 per day
Estimated number of direct URL entries per month = 16 *30
= c. 480 per month (1)

The estimates for mistyping/misspelling rates and direct URL entry rates will vary depending upon the length of the name, its memorability and its complexity. However, the 10 % proportions assumed above are useful and rather conservative indicators of the general magnitude of the issue.

For example, a European energy supply company has confirmed they get three times as much traffic via their various branded domain names than through Google searches. In other words, people typically access their site by typing the name directly into the URL bar rather than searching for it. If someone else owns those addresses, whether coincidentally or maliciously, then those users are not going to receive the experience that the company would like them to have. If we use that factor of 300 % instead of 10 % in the GN Netcom calculation above, then the company is missing out on potentially 1,700 visits per month.

It is difficult to locate information on URL mistyping and misspelling rates. The 10 % mistyping/misspelling estimate we have used here is based on research by Potter [44], who looked at entry error rates in an aircraft flight management system. He found that the 10 % error rate was generally consistent for all data entry, but could also rise substantially under increased workload. In other words, the greater the stress or pressure, the greater the error rate.

As can be seen from Fig. 2.3, there are different links to other websites. One of the links is for Plantronics, a direct competitor. From the brand owner's point of view, this can be thought of as a virtual version of a shopping mall, where you own a McDonald's concession and put signs in are following the signs to McDonalds, but you end up at Burger King instead.

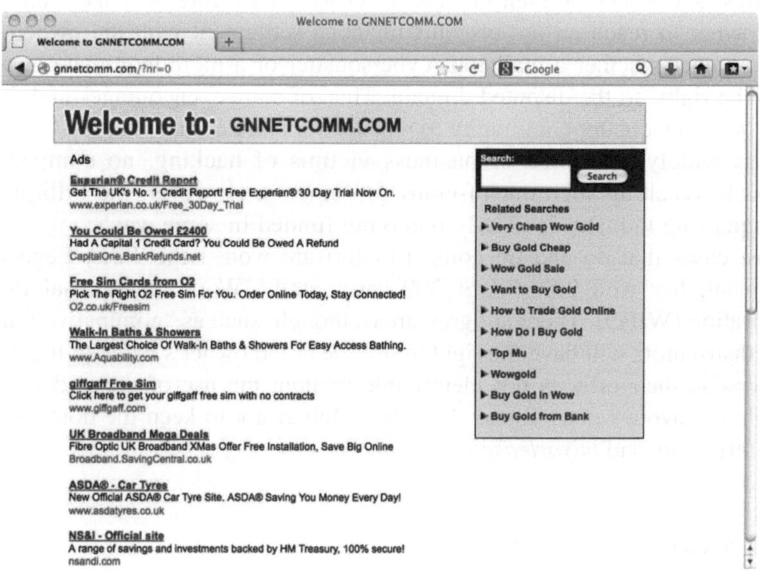

Fig. 2.3 GN Netcom's website is www.gnnetcom.com. This is what www.gnnetcom.com looks like. There is no reference to GN Netcom anywhere on the page

Sometimes, users can end up at the wrong destination because of simple confusion over the domain name used by a brand. For example, in Copenhagen there is a mass transit system called the Metro. There is also a newspaper with the same name. When a person types www.metro.dk into a URL bar of a browser, it is not clear whether they will get information about a newspaper or about a train service. A sizeable portion of users will end up disgruntled either way because they will not get the information that they are looking for and will have to expend additional effort to modify their search behaviour and try an alternative method.

In a recent study, antivirus company Sophos estimated that 80 % of mistyped URLs lead to typosquatting sites. The authors of the report calculated all possible single character entry errors for a number of famous brands and then saw how many of those error URLs were registered. For the most famous brands, that rate was up to 86 % of single character error variations on their URLs. Furthermore, they found that 2.7 % of the typosquatting sites fell under the general category of "cybercrime," supporting activities such as hacking, phishing and spamming. A further 2.4 % were adult or dating sites. 33 % of sites were advertising sites, either selling products (potentially direct competitor products to those of the targeted brand owner) or generic IT or search services [21].

Domain name monetisation is serious business estimated to be worth US$1 billion per year. In the cybersquatting communities, registration of branded domain names is considered as an effective and rewarding business model.

The calculation is very straightforward. It typically costs US$6.95 to register a *.com* domain name, with no questions asked other than an ability to pay. It costs a brand owner a minimum of US$1,500 to raise a legal dispute. Litigation is costly, and cases take weeks or even months to resolve. Therefore, it makes sense for a brand owner to reach an out-of-court financial settlement with the owner of the domain name (whether a malicious cybersquatter or a more legitimate owner) to secure the rights to the disputed domain. This, of course, encourages and, indeed, funds the cybersquatter community to register yet more domain names.

As is widely suspected of business victims of hacking, no company will confess to reaching such out-of-court settlements. However, the billion-dollar cybersquatting industry is clearly receiving funded in some way.

Most cases that do end up going to court are won. Lego Juris, Lego's legal department, has won 299 out of 300 cases at the World Intellectual Property Organisation (WIPO). There are grey areas, though, such as "nominative fair use", where distributors will have the right to use the brand owner's name in the domain, as otherwise their offer is not identifiable without the use of the trademark. An example is Toyota versus Tabari [9], where Tabari got to keep the domain names *buy-a-lexus.com* and *buyorleaselexus.com*.

2.3.1.3 Social Media User Names

A social media username is the domain name on social networks, such as *facebook.com/cocacola*. In 2009, Facebook made it possible to edit the user name of your profile on Facebook, and most social networks offer this possibility today. Facebook, with 955 million users currently, is by far the most popular social network at the time of writing. In 2010, it was reported that an average user was spending an incredible 55 min daily on Facebook [25]. A more recent study in Sweden showed men using Facebook for an average of 64 min per day and women using it for 81 min every day. Furthermore, the study found that the users logged in on average 6.1 times every day and 70 % went to Facebook as part of their regular logon routine whenever they started their computer. Perhaps even more surprisingly, 26 % of the respondents admitted to feeling symptoms of withdrawal if they had not logged on recently [19]. Such habitual behaviour means that social media outlets such as Facebook represent a significant opportunity for advertising and revenue generation from a fairly captive market.

Consequently, brands have started to focus on social media. In 2010, Google incorporated social media results into its search results. For example, if you make an Internet search for Pepsi, four of the top 10 results are from social media networks: Twitter, Google+, YouTube and Facebook.

Social media user names are the new domain names for brand owners. They represent additional opportunities for building a dialogue with consumers. In 2011 at the Super Bowl, the most viewed TV event in the US, both Pepsi and Budweiser directed viewers to their Facebook pages instead of their main websites.

There is no equivalent to WIPO for social media usernames. At the same time, individuals can have the same rights to a name as the brand owner, so the brand will have no special rights of ownership of the social media user names. This affected Maggi, a top 200 global brand with a turnover of over US$100 million, which had to settle for a less obvious address than *Facebook.com/maggi*, which was owned by a person called, quite coincidentally, Maggi. This is similar to the difficulty faced by Sting in his failed attempt to secure *sting.com* discussed in Chap. 1.

Since the domain name market is more mature and companies have had time to establish their "traditional" web sites, it is usually straightforward to find a company or brand home page via an Internet search engine such as Google or Yahoo. However, social media presence is not as established and stable as for the more traditional sites. Furthermore, the search engines used within social media networks are not set up to support brand names as explicitly. There is far less prioritisation of results. Thus, while the search results are more "democratic" in the sense that anyone can work their way into the results list, this represents a challenge to a brand owner who wants to direct potential customers to the official brand. As an example, a user searching for "Lego" on Facebook's internal search engine will find multiple responses, many of which feature Lego's logo—see Fig. 2.4. Finding Lego's official page is thus much more complex than searching via an Internet search engine. This example indicates how important it is to have the "correct" username.

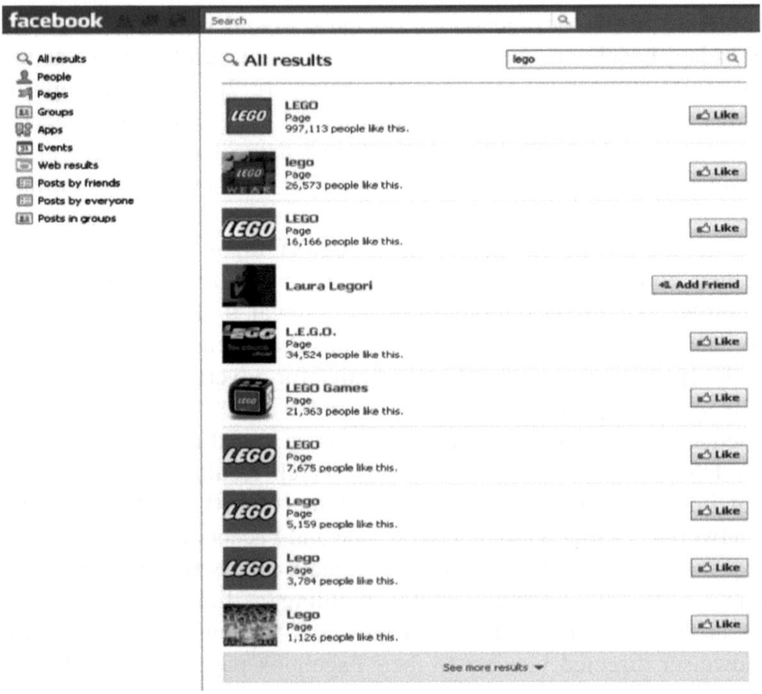

Fig. 2.4 Searching for the official Lego page on Facebook

Twitter in particular is suffering from brandjacking activities and there seems to be a black market for these addresses. The state of Israel paid a significant amount to get *twitter.com/israel*. Danske Spil, the principal gaming company in Denmark, also had their name taken.

2.3.1.4 Logos

Logos are the visual trademarks on the Internet. Trademarks are protected in geographical areas. However the Internet has no geographical limits, so confusingly similar, yet wholly legal, trademarks will potentially confuse customers.

2.3.1.5 Presence Risk

Consistency in branding is a golden rule of marketing. Different messages will confuse customers and damage the brand. The Internet enables the brand owner to build up sales channels via affiliates and distributors. However if there is not a strict contract in place, or if partners do not behave according to generally accepted conduct, then it will compromise the brand. Affiliates will typically give their loyalty to the brand where they can make most profit, unless there are other brand attributes that they strongly identify with. So the most well known brands can be used as storefront to attract visitors, but as soon as they enter the shop, the affiliate will offer them another brand. At the same time the brand owner can end up competing directly with affiliates. This can happen on the Internet through searches, such as at Google where customers of its Adwords service can often find themselves competing against affiliated companies for the same advertising space. 88.8 % of the global web traffic [31] comes via Google. That is where most customers will come from, so it is not surprising that similar companies offering similar products, sometimes even the same products, can find themselves competing in the same space.

2.3.1.6 Paid Placement

Hotel booking is a competitive industry, where the use of affiliates and other intermediaries is common. Markmonitor revealed that the top five global hotel chains miss out on an estimated 580 million clicks annually [36], clicks which were diverted instead to affiliates and sometimes even competitors. The affiliates were paid US$300 million in extra commission for these clicks. US$1.9 billion of turnover was diverted to rival hotels. Common methods of traffic diversion were cybersquatting and typosquatting (registering brands' domain names with and without spelling errors), using brand names as keywords to appear in paid search advertisements and by ranking in the organic search results for these hotel brands. One domain name alone diverted 3 million users.

When you make a Google search, the small advertisements displayed at the top and to the right are from Google Adwords. Adwords operates by asking companies to bid for the right to appear in the Adwords results for specific search terms, such as "hotels" in this case. The company only pays, though, if the user clicks on the Advertisment words result. If the user does not click on the advertisement, though, then the company is not charged for this service.

The company that bids the most amount will rank at the top of the Adwords results and thus at the top of the main search results as well. Popular advertisers will pay less to rank higher, effectively getting a bulk-buying discount. A top rank in a highly competitive market can cost as much as US$5–10 per click, while no competition for a keyword costs no more than US$0.10 per click. So when an affiliate is competing with a brand owner on Adwords, the click price will go up, and the brand owner pays a premium charge to obtain a higher rank.

This raises the interesting question of whether it is legal for competitors to rank for others' registered trademarks. In 2010, Louis Vuitton (LV) took Google to court and claimed that they were liable for allowing competitors to rank for LV's trademarks. The court ruling favoured LV and set a precedent that now allows brand owners to request Google to block others from ranking for their registered trademarks. However, Google is not giving up on this lucrative market, defending their position as the "Yellow Pages of the Internet." Our research shows that while Google disallows

Table 2.2 The monthly volume of searches performed using Google searching for the Marriott hotel in Copenhagen

Table	Estimated monthly volume
Marriott hotel Copenhagen	4.400
Marriott Copenhagen	9.900
Marriott hotels Copenhagen	2.900
Marriott København	3.600
Hotel Marriott København	1.600
Total	22.400

the use of the trademark directly (in this case "Marriott"), advertisements still appear when the trademark is only one of the keywords in a search phrase. The upshot of this is that if you look for a hotel in Copenhagen using the more specific search "Marriott hotel Copenhagen," then other hotel chains will be included in the search results.

A Google search for "Marriott hotel Copenhagen" using quotation marks to specify that the returned results will only include results containing all of the search words will show a highly competitive search term, where Marriott should be alone, as shown in Fig. 2.4.

Marriott ranks at the top of the search, but several intermediaries and competitors push up the price that has to be paid by Marriott to occupy that position in the Google Adwords economy. So Marriott has to pay a premium price. According to Google's keyword tool, Table 2.2 shows the estimated monthly search volume for relevant search terms.

Google's traffic estimator concludes that a top rank will cost approximately US$2.50 per click. If Marriott is paying a surcharge of US$2.40 for each click and 20 % of all users click on their ad (standard), then they pay the following extra charge for Google Adwords per year:

$$\begin{aligned}&22,400\,\text{(total searches)} \times 20\,\%\,\text{(Adwords clicks)} \times 12\,\text{(months)}\\&\quad = 53,760\,\text{clicks per year}\\&53,760 \times (2.50\,\text{(price per click)} - 0.10\,\text{(price if no other bidder)})\\&\quad = \text{US}\,\$129,024\,\text{per year}\end{aligned} \tag{2}$$

It must, of course, be remembered that the Google search engine does provide significant customer traffic to the owners of many businesses. This is clearly a valuable resource to the business community as a whole. However, it must also be noted that any trademark owner has a right to challenge Google's returned results if they discover that other companies, such as direct competitors, rank in the returned search results for their particular brand names.

On a side note, these calculations show how important it is to actually have a trademark and to protect it properly. Norwegian Air Shuttle, the airline company, does not have a trademark registration for the word "Norwegian." They pay an astonishing US$1.4 million per year solely to bid on their brand name in Denmark. Appendix 1 explains how we arrive at this estimate.

Facebook's advertising network is called Facebook Ads. These are small advertisement boxes that users can see on the right side on their Facebook page.

According to Emarketer, Facebook Ads brought in an estimated US$1.25 billion in the first three months of 2013, with 25 % of that revenue coming from advertising on mobile platforms, i.e. smartphones and tablets [4]. Advertisements have to be approved by Facebook, but there appears to be no obvious brand control. In a famous incident in 2011, auction site *GrabSwag.com* brandjacked *Dealzon.com*, to attract visitors. *GrabSwag.com* posted an advertisement offering an iPad 2 for only US$11.73. However, rather than posting it under their own name, they used a user name of *dealzon.com*. The company effectively masqueraded as one of their competitors. Unsuspecting customers clicked on the link to find that instead of being offered a brand new iPad 2 from one company, they were being invited to bid on a second hand one from a wholly different company [10].

2.3.1.7 Search Engine Manipulation

Organic search results are the natural search results that appear on the left side in the search engine, i.e. those that are not paid for via the Adwords function. The majority of users will click on the results on the first page of returned results. Consequently, these positions are very competitive. Often, the first few results of a search that are not clearly connected to the brand owner have used so-called black hat methods, i.e. methods not approved by Google, to rank higher up the search results. Such methods can include adding other brands' names and reference in text that is hidden to the user, but can be found by search engine crawlers. These crawlers are automated programmes that are used by search engines to follow all links and text on a page to build a map of information that is available on the Internet.

The data collection methods used by the crawlers are very sophisticated and they allow the search engines to perform the calculations necessary to provide the ranked list of search results to a particular search query. For example, a page is more likely to be placed higher in the list if a word is repeated several times. Additionally, pages that are directly referenced from multiple other pages and domains are weighted more highly than pages with only one external link to them. Knowing how the crawlers work and how the search engines adjust their calculations based on the data collected, it is possible to gain a higher search position by gaming the system, such as deliberately building several domains that reference each other extensively to make pages appear to be more widely referenced (and thus deemed "better" by the search engines) than they actually are.

Google's secret algorithms select what is most relevant for the visitors. According to Rand Fishkin from SEOmoz, one of the most acknowledged SEO consultants, at least 55 % of traffic to Google goes to the top three organic search results. It is therefore important that brands appear in the top three for their brand terms instead of having affiliates and other parties occupy these positions. It is very tempting to use black hat methods to rank higher, but Google will penalize such acts, if detected, and the brand will lose its ranking. This happened to BMW some years ago when they used a very creative agency to increase its profile in web searches. This is a form of brand risk where the risk has come from within the company through a failure to follow appropriate procedures, in this case Google's own mandated procedures.

2.3.1.8 Spam

Spam is the common term for unwanted e-mails sent out indiscriminately to as many recipients as possible in mass mailings. Such spam messages serve to generate revenue for the spammers who send the message out. In 2007, 95 % of all e-mails sent were spam. However, by 2011 e-mail spam had been reduced to 72 % of all e-mails [48]. This is not because spammers were being sent to jail. Some of the reduction is because the Internet has become a lot better at policing itself. There are companies and organisations, such as SpamHaus, that are dedicated to the eradication of spam. However, much of the decrease is because of a change of tactics by the spammers. They have been migrating across to social networks, such as Twitter and Facebook, where the necessary volume of traffic exists to make spamming a profitable activity and where conditions are ideal.

The revenue generation for spammers can be via a number of methods, such as phishing, selling illegal or counterfeit products, or the infamous 419 scam, named after the Nigerian Law outlawing such activity. The 419 e-mail scam was one of the earliest forms of spam observed. The spammer would often pretend to be a senior military officer or government official who had access to a large sum of money, but needed "help" from someone overseas to move the money to a "safe" location. The trick was that the "safe" location would often require a deposit to open the necessary account and so the victim of the scam was instructed to deposit a sum of, say, US$10,000 in order for the scammer to be able to transfer a much larger sum. Of course, once the deposit was made, the scammer would empty the bank account and disappear. Worryingly, anecdotal evidence has suggested that this scam worked best when sent to bank managers, who probably felt that they had been contacted because of their occupation.

As Internet users have become more aware of such scams, the spammers moved to offering illegal or counterfeit products, especially pharmaceutical ones. Medications such as Viagra are commonly offered for sale at a fraction of the retail price. Unsuspecting customers will either find their credit card details being used for fraudulent purposes or else useless sugar pills arriving by post.

Spammers have since modified their activities to arguably the most dangerous and pernicious form yet, the phishing e-mail. Phishing is an attempt to acquire sensitive information such as user names, passwords and credit card details by masquerading as a trustworthy entity (a company or a person) in an e-mail. Brands are the trust-builder that spammers use as a Trojan horse. They rely on users lowering their guard when they see a brand name that they know and trust in the phishing e-mail. Typical phishing e-mails masquerade as being from major high street banks, credit card companies or money transfer services, such as Western Union. However, phishing e-mails can also purport to be from courier services needing a customs or import duty payment for a valuable shipment (a variant on the 419 scam) or a customer survey offering a free prize in return for personal details.

The most common advice given for brand owners to avoid the more common spam scams is to always use confidential personal identifiers in the e-mail that are not readily available in the public domain. Banks and credit card companies typically do this by including, for example, 4 digits of the account or card number.

Should a victim click on a link in a phishing e-mail then a variety of unpleasant consequences can ensue. These consequences can include the automatic installation of malware on the victim's computer, which can include viruses, Trojan horses, key loggers, trackers or applications that pop adverts up on the screen every few minutes. Alternatively, the phishing e-mails may contain a link to a web page that purports to be the login screen for the victim's bank. The victim is then encouraged to log on to their bank account. Unknown to them, their login information is then stored by the owner of the fake site, who will typically also be the originator of the phishing e-mail. A technical error, such as "Service temporarily not available—please try again later" is then displayed on the screen. While the victim waits to try again, the owner of the fake web page will have unfettered access to the victim's bank or credit card information.

Phishing e-mails used to be straightforward to detect. Commonly they would include spelling mistakes or the URLs of the web pages would be clearly fraudulent. However, as the intended victims have become more savvy about identifying phishing attempts, the phishers have become more sophisticated in their attempts at deception. The URLs used, for example, often now include the name of the brand that they are trying to hide behind, for example http://www.fedex.com.tr/...

Such practices are not only harmful to the victims, who can end up losing thousands from their bank accounts, but also the brand owners who, rightly or wrongly, get associated in the user's psyche with the phishing attempts. Many brand owners now use explicit personal identifiers unique to their individual customers, such as their name and postal code, in an attempt to differentiate legitimate e-mails for phishing attempts.

The security consulting company [16] estimates that a typical phishing attack, where access to a bank account is obtained, will cost US$1,800 per victim (1 victim per 2000 spammed) and the brand owner will lose US$400 for each employee's extra time spend to solve this problem. Additionally there is damage to the corporate reputation, which leads to future lack of trust and loss in customer satisfaction. The research for this book did not find any hard evidence of turnover loss due to damage to the brand's reputation. However there are plenty of unhappy victims letting off steam in the forums blaming the brand owners for not warning them more actively about scams.

As mentioned earlier spammers have shifted to social media with Starbucks gift cards being one of the latest victims [42]. Facebook users have been invited to complete a form to receive a free US$40 gift card from Starbucks. However, it appears that this offer is simply a vehicle for the spread of malware.

Social media arguably relies more on trust that any other media. According to Steve [35], social networks such as Facebook, MySpace, Orkut, LinkedIn and Twitter have significant security gaps. They are attractive for those with malicious intent given the rich user details such as login details and other extensive personal data that is readily available to those with the right skills to exploit the security holes. Users do not have the same defence mechanisms as elsewhere on the Internet because of the fundamental ethos of social media being based around increased sharing of information. Brands will lose customer trust if they are used as a Trojan horse via their social media presence.

Given that a Twitter update can only have 140 characters, short URL services like *bit.ly* were invented, where typical URLs are compressed into codes that computers can understand, but people cannot. They are ideal for spammers given that the link does not serve as a complete road sign, as can be seen in Fig. 2.5 from a Lego tweet. This reduced information means that users cannot assess the provenance of a link without clicking on it and seeing where they end up. This is a significant reduction in security for users compared with the ability to see full URLs in a typical e-mail.

The Twitter update shown in Fig. 2.6, though, leads to a nonsensical blog and a suspicious-looking outlet store that does not reveal its contents unless you first register on the site.

It is unrealistic to expect all potential users to be able to tell the difference between genuine and malicious links from the information available in these two figures. Consequently, it is imperative that brand owners develop effective means

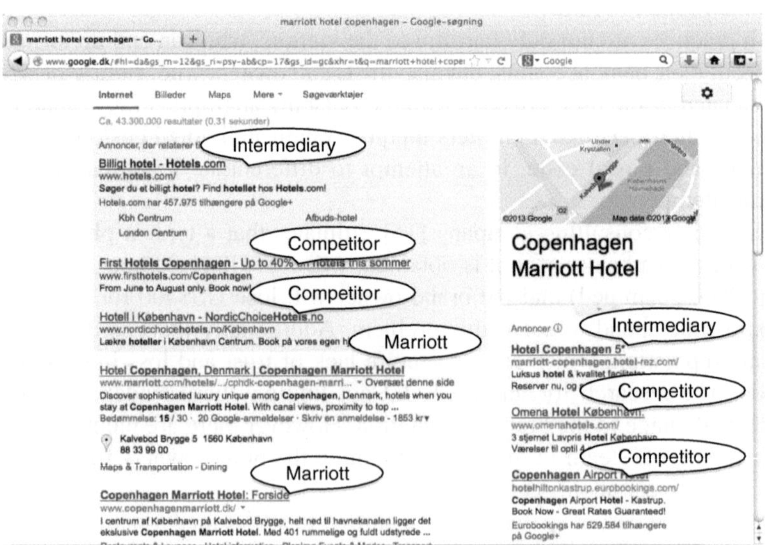

Fig. 2.5 Google search for “Marriott hotel Copenhagen”

Fig. 2.6 Genuine Twitter links from Lego

to identify and control the risk to themselves and their customers when using social media (Fig. 2.7).

2.3.1.9 Equity Risk

Brand equity reflects the functional and emotional benefits of the brand perceived by the company's customers. The brand's customers' emotional drivers can also, in particular circumstances, be the biggest brand risks. Emotional drivers are not

Fig. 2.7 Unsafe Twitter link

permanent and can change over time. Apple used to rely on the late Steve Jobs' personal charisma. A celebrity endorsement, such as Tiger Woods, can make or break a brand. According to Chris Knittel and Victor Stango, Professors of Economics at the University of California at Davis, the stock prices of the seven companies that have or had sponsorship deals with Tiger Woods lost US$12 billion in market value in the month after the scandal surrounding his personal life was reported in the news [33]. A curious discovery in their study was that their competitors' turnover grew as a consequence of this incident.

Brand owners have to react quickly when emotional drivers associated with their brands become less favourable and in extreme circumstances may even turn on them. It requires constant monitoring on the Internet to pick up any changes in sentiment as quickly as possible to allow time for the brand to either respond or to develop a new strategy.

2.3.1.10 Counterfeiting

Counterfeiting is a double problem for brand owners. First, there is a direct loss of revenue as customers inadvertently purchase fraudulent copies, generating income for the counterfeiters instead of the legitimate brand owners. Second, if the market is flooded with cheap, and often inferior, copies then the sense of cachet and exclusivity associated with a brand is diminished. This can lead to a cancerous destruction of a brand's reputation if left unchecked.

The counterfeiting business on the Internet is huge. In 2004, the International Chamber of Commerce (ICC) launched an initiative to raise awareness of this issue—Business Action to Stop Counterfeiting and Piracy (BASCAP). BASCAP estimates that the trade in counterfeit and pirated products is worth up to US$650 billion per year globally, with the expectation that this might rise to US$1.7 trillion by 2015 [3]. There is also strong evidence that counterfeiting and piracy is closely connected with organised crime [2].

Three product categories alone (computers, apparel and consumer electronics) represented 44 % of online sales (US$67.6 billion) in 2009 making them very attractive for counterfeiting [49].

At a company level the problems of counterfeiting can be highly damaging. Zippo, the lighter company, estimates that the 12 million lighters they produce annually is only half the number actually being sold that purports to be genuine Zippo products [41]. This is a real problem as the quality of the fakes is improving to the point where even Zippo employees have difficulties spotting the difference when they are returned for repair under Zippo's guarantee.

It is highly problematic to identify whether a product is counterfeit on the Internet. It is often not easy in the physical world, but on the Internet users often only have two out of the six cues from the physical world—price and purchase point [46]. Counterfeiters can further obscure this by setting a price close to the original. The other common cues are physical: the packaging, labelling, quality and difference in brand name.

The other cue, purchase point, can also be solved simply: copy substantial portions of the real website! This copying often includes the logo, font, background colour, etc., anything that connects the fake site to the genuine one in the mind of the customer.

As we have discussed earlier, brand owners who suffer counterfeiting have a direct economic loss. However, studies have shown that there are also long-term consequences regarding lost brand loyalty. This is true especially in luxury products, where a customer's incentive is often to buy something no one else has [14]. This leads to the obvious question of what brand owners should do to limit counterfeiting. A study in Brazil and the US [50] concluded that brand owners need to be active in educating customers about the risks of counterfeit products, the benefit of the original product and how to obtain the genuine product. Another study [12] supported this conclusion and recommended that distributors, employees and other channel members should be educated by the brand owner. The study further concluded that end customers should be able to track official distributors of the brand and recognize when the website offers original products [46].

2.3.1.11 Digital Piracy

Digital technology and the ubiquity of the Internet have increased the ease with which quality graphics, text, audio, video and software can be copied and widely distributed. When a brand's value proposition centres around digital assets then digital piracy has to be considered a real threat and arguably even the principal threat to a brand's value. Brand owners who suffer digital piracy are typically from industries such as music, film, software, information and literature. The International Federation of the Phonographic Industry (IFPI) claims that 34 % of all recorded music products sold worldwide in 2004 were pirated copies and that piracy costs the industry over US300 billion between 2008 and 2015 [28]. 1.2 million jobs are expected to be lost in the European creative industries alone due to digital piracy in that same period.

The music and film industries have coordinated public campaigns against digital piracy, and violators have been prosecuted to scare others from going the same way. The early evidence suggests that this approach is having a tangible effect [26]. New legal business models have appeared in the process. For example, Spotify is a monthly subscription service where customers pay a fixed monthly fee to get unlimited access to music.

2.3.1.12 Grey Markets

Original brand products can make their way to the customers through unauthorized dealers and business partners in violation of the original distribution agreements. This is known as a grey market. Grey markets on the Internet are very difficult to control for brand owners, who think that they can keep the distribution channels apart. Grey market products are almost always sold at a lower price. Estimates of the size of international grey markets range from US$7 billion to US$10 billion [37]. A subsequent study showed it was unclear whether consumers were better or worse off in the long term by parallel import [22]. However, there was a clear indication that significant brand value was lost over time.

2.3.1.13 Reputation Risk

When a company fails to deliver according to expectations, then its brand's reputation is damaged. Risk to brand reputation can be divided into two categories, firstly when companies do not comply with established regulation, and secondly when the company does not live up to the ethical expectations. Product safety issues, environmental hazards, etc., are typical reputation risk cases. Joel Podolny [43], an American sociologist, opines that reputation is:

> an expectation of some behaviour or behaviours based on past demonstrations of those same behaviours.

According to Podolny, a reputation can only be gained over time. It is an attractive position to obtain, yet also very fragile, as a great reputation will enable the company to set a premium price for their products, but can be potentially irrevocably damaged very quickly, as in the Gerald Ratner example mentioned earlier.

Traditionally a company's Public Relations Department would handle the corporate reputation. However, with the growth of social media, reputation management has become increasingly difficult to control using traditional approaches. [18] found that 74 % of employees surveyed believe it is easy to damage a brand's reputation via sites such as Facebook, Twitter and YouTube. At the same time, only 15 % of executives surveyed said that reputational risk and social media are boardroom issues. This indicates that, at present, brand risk on social media is not on the radar of many company boards.

2.3.1.14 Rumours

This potential for damaging a brand via social media is exemplified by the threat of rumours on the Internet and the damage they can do to a brand's reputation. Anyone can start an anonymous rumour on the Internet. As it is difficult to validate the trustworthiness of Internet sources and with the almost instantaneous speed of distribution of social media, almost any brand is vulnerable. Such rumours can be about financial irregularities, customer complaints, product defects or unethical business practices.

Such rumours usually come from someone with a metaphorical axe to grind with the company, such as a dissatisfied (ex) employee, a disgruntled customer, a competitor, an investor in the company or a former CEO. In many cases, the risk originates at some point from inside the company being targeted. In 2009, two employees from Domino's Pizza uploaded a video to YouTube [7] where they filmed a prank video of themselves stuffing cheese in their noses and then in a customer's sandwich. The video went viral at an impressive speed. The two videos on YouTube got more than 1 million views before they were shut down. The brand's reputation was severely damaged almost immediately and has proven to be very durable damage. At the time of writing, two years after the incident, it still appears in the top search results on YouTube for *Domino's Pizza,* ranked above their own positive public relations material. It must be noted that YouTube is the second most popular search engine in the world. This was very serious damage.

Brand risk can even come directly from a brand's own management team. In 2011, Bob Parsons, the CEO of GoDaddy—the worldwide market leader in domain names, released a video from his elephant hunt in Zimbabwe. Originally thought as self-promotion, it ended up with a PETA campaign against GoDaddy requesting customers to close down their account [47].

Competitors were quick to take advantage of this mistake. NameCheap, a direct competitor, invited GoDaddy customers to transfer their domain names, offering to donate US$1 for each customer who transferred to them to Save The Elephants [52]. 20,000 domain names were transferred within 24 h [8]. In 1 week, approximately 100,000 domains were transferred away, leaving GoDaddy with an estimated loss of US$5 million [5]. That was clearly a very expensive holiday trip for Mr Parsons.

Rebecca Herold, a security consultant, recommends that companies have a social media policy in place to ensure employees do not give away competitive intelligence and customer information when tweeting or updating their Facebook status [45]. This might, on the surface, appear to be obvious advice, but some users tend to forget just how public the digital domain really is. While the intention of the poster of a juicy bit of gossip may simply be to alert close friends to something new, a quick re-tweet to a more public page by just one recipient of the original post can lead to the message "going viral" and spreading rapidly and completely out of control.

2.3.1.15 User Complaints

While rumours can have a strong effect on reputation, another serious risk to brand reputation is customer complaints. When customers feel let down by the company, then the Internet has made it possible for them to simultaneously let off steam and get some measure of "revenge." Copulsky describes the three stages of losing a customer's trust [15], p. 74:

1. Disappointment: The customer does not receive the expected brand experience
2. Anger: The company fails to address the customer's disappointment
3. Rage: Customers react publicly.

Public reaction can be via comments on blogs, social networks or customer review sites. More organized attacks are websites and Facebook groups specially set up to target and channel ill-feeling about a particular brand. These sites tend to obtain high ranks in search engine results, as they share many of the same key words as the corporate sites of the brand owner's and often have lots of support from likeminded customers. Remember, the more links to a web page, the higher that page ranks on the search engine results. Thus, if lots of individual users link to a particular page or review, then that page will score more highly in the next web search. This can quickly become self-supporting. More links mean more users find the page, which means more users will be able to link to it and so on. YouTube videos are especially easy to link to, are often very popular and are now integrated in the search engine search results.

Brand owners have to be aware of this kind of rage and have strategies in place for dealing with it. According to Copulsky, reading through online reviews and ratings prior to a purchase is a critical step for most customers today ([15], p. 83) and bad reviews carry more weight than good reviews. One reason for this discrepancy in weight is that many consumers are aware that some companies put out fake positive reviews of their own products and there is no reliable way to check the authenticity of a review to ensure it came from a genuine consumer. The corollary of this is that a bad review may be considered more likely to have come from a real person and thus be considered to be more reliable. The irony of this situation is that companies can exploit this perception to promote their own brand by posting negative reviews of their competitors. This phenomenon is often seen with political parties using newspaper comments sections to rubbish their rivals' policies while pretending to be a typical voter.

There is an effective method for dealing with customer rage, though. A study conducted by Harris Interactive on behalf of Oracle, showed that when brand owners reacted to unhappy customers, a majority of these customers responded positively and even deleted their negative comments [24]. Bo Kyung Kim concludes that negative messages on Facebook and Twitter increased the general negative reputation of an organization and were therefore more likely to result in boycotts of the company's products [27].

Winter and Steger [53] argue that brand owners should only react after considering how plausible the activist arguments are, from whom they came and how media friendly the story is. A judgement needs to be made for deciding on a response. Sometimes a public denial can simply add fuel to a particular fire that was going to die out on its own. Brand owners need to assess carefully whether an intervention is required or whether it might potentially do more harm than good.

As part of a social media policy, it is important that employees know how to act on social media, where they may be considered a spokesperson of the company, even if that is not their official role. To ensure consistency in public communications, companies such as Kodak, Yahoo and Coca-Cola have added employee social media policies into their general business conduct principles. Gatorade's Mission Control Center could be a future scenario for most brand owners. They follow conversations on social media round the clock, with the objective of monitoring online discussions, tracking brand attributes, monitoring the sports landscape, tracking media performance, sorting trends and following the "buzz." If someone talks about Gatorade, they will know about it almost instantly and they will know how to react. Applied Research [11] confirms that companies' fear of engaging in social media is real. 28 % of the respondents had suffered damage to their brand through social media.

2.3.1.16 Status Risk

While brand reputation is associated with particular products, status risk is the parent company's overall reputation. The company's reputation can affect the brand reputation both positively and negatively. Having a high company status can sometimes be the deciding factor when a customer has to make a purchasing decision. When a product is not fully understood by the customer, the customer will sometimes put his or her trust in the company's reputation instead. Sometimes, this could be a high-tech product with complicated specifications, but even judging the quality of a bottle of wine can be complex.

Companies with high status can be affected negatively when associated with a low status company [43]. When a supplier requests the use of the brand logo on their website, it is important to consider the public perception of the association that may be formed. In other words, selling a premium brand in a discount supermarket may temporarily increase sales, but may also cheapen the perceived value of the brand.

Customer testimonials are highly influential in the purchase decision, especially if the brands associated are well known. Therefore it is tempting for some companies to do something under the radar to be associated with a well-known brand to benefit from the golden halo effect of the premium brands. Where this is a genuinely earned relationship, then the premium brand owner usually will not mind. However, sometimes companies just put logos on their site where there is no established relationship simply to piggyback on the premium brand's reputation. The premium brand may then be exposed to the "cheapening" effect described earlier and so this represents another form of brand risk.

2.3.1.17 Market Risk

Even a strong brand can end up in a declining market. Changing attitudes to consumption of a product, for example tobacco-related products, will expose the brand to risk. This is what is known as market risk. Even if a brand has good equity, reputation and status it can still end up in a market segment that is declining in volume. Apart from customer motivation, legal constraints are another risk factor to consider. On the Internet, marketers have a unique opportunity to detect early changing customer attitudes. Yes, there are pitfalls engaging on social media, however maintaining a conversation with their customers on the Internet will enable the company to adapt to a changing climate.

Table 2.3 Sources of costs of brand risks

Table	In US$ million
Phishing	3.200
Domain/Paid placement	1.000
Secondary domain names	17.5
Online counterfeiting	137.000
Total	141.000

2.3.2 Summary of Brand Risks

In this chapter, we have identified many of the typical online brand risks facing a brand owner. The likelihood of a brand risk depends on the industry in which the brand is found and the nature of the products associated with the brand. There is a wide variation in the nature of the threats and the potential consequences of each threat. However, there is one area of commonality for all brand owners in all circumstances, which is that being proactive is essential. Being proactive can avoid later costs, which will be several times higher than the initial investment. Proactivity makes sense in all aspects from acquiring the correct domain names in time, to monitoring Adwords for competitors ranking on a keyword to help your customers avoid the typical scams. Furthermore, minimising reaction time to a potential threat is essential when defending against a brand risk, especially when it comes to retaining customer trust. Another common factor is the difficulty in estimating the actual brand damage. While there is often an obvious immediate direct cost, the damage to the reputation is often impossible to measure. MarkMonitor estimates direct costs of brand risk to be more than US$141 billion annually [38]. They divide these numbers as shown in Table 2.3.

Counterfeiting on the Internet is by far the most expensive brand risk, so any company has to be aware of this. However again, these are general numbers, and do not necessarily reflect any specific brand owner's situation.

Having examined the nature of risks to brands, in the next chapter we will explore possible methods for managing those risks.

References

1. Abrahams, D.: Brand Risk—adding risk literacy to brand management. Gower Publishing, UK (2008)
2. AACAP: Proving the connection: links between intellectual property theft and organised crime. Alliance Against Counterfeiting and Piracy (AACAP). http://www.allianceagainstiptheft.co.uk/downloads/reports/Proving-the-Connection.pdf (2002)
3. BASCAP: Estimating the global economic and social impacts of counterfeiting and piracy. http://www.iccwbo.org/Data/Documents/Bascap/Global-Impacts-Study-Full-Report/ (2011). Accessed Feb 2011
4. BBC: Facebook profits from mobile advertising. http://www.bbc.co.uk/news/business-22376553 (2013). Accessed 2 May 2013

5. Berkens, M.: Total damage to Godaddy from Parsons elephant shooting? About 100,000 domains. The Domains. http://www.thedomains.com/2011/04/15/total-damage-from-parsons-elephant-shooting-about-100000-domains/ (2011). Accessed 15 April 2011
6. Berner, R.: P&G: Razing rivals with Gillette? Business Week. http://www.businessweek.com/stories/2005-01-27/p-and-g-razing-rivals-with-gillette (2005). Accessed 27 Jan 2005
7. Blodget, H.: Domino's YouTube nightmare. Business Insider. http://www.businessinsider.com/henry-blodget-dominos-2009-4 (2009). Accessed 16 April 2009
8. Brian, M.: Namecheap raises US$20 k for save the elephants following GoDaddy CEO's hunt video. The Next Web. http://thenextweb.com/insider/2011/04/05/namecheap-raises-20k-for-save-the-elephants-following-godaddy-ceos-hunt-video/ (2011). Accessed 5 April 2011
9. Brody, P.M., Roberts, A.J.: What's in a domain name? nominative fair use online after Toyota vs. Tabari. Trademark Reporter **100**(6), 1290–1334 (2010)
10. Carr, A.: Unchecked spam ads infiltrate Facebook, hijack Dealzon brand. Fast Company. htt p://www.fastcompany.com/1771099/unchecked-spam-ads-infiltrate-facebook-hijack-dealzon-brand (2011a). Accessed 4 Aug 2011
11. Carr, DF.: Could social media flub cost you US$4.3 million? InformationWeek. http://www.informationweek.co.uk/social-business/news/industry_analysis/could-social-media-flub-cost-you-43-mill/231002459 (2011b). Accessed 25 July 2011
12. Chaudhry, P., Zimmerman, A., Peters, J., Cordell, V.: Preserving intellectual property rights: managerial insight into the escalating counterfeit market quandary. Bus. Horiz. **52**(1), 57–66 (2009)
13. Christensen, B M.: KFC 'Genetically manipulated organisms' hoax. Hoax-Slayer.com. http://www.hoax-slayer.com/kfc-fake-chickens-hoax.shtml (2013)
14. Commuri, S.: The impact of counterfeiting on genuine-item consumers' brand relationships. J. Mark. **73**(3), 86–98 (2009)
15. Copulsky, J.: Brand resilience—managing risk and recovery in a high-speed world. Palgrave Macmillan, New York (2011)
16. Cyveillance: The cost of phishing: understanding the true cost dynamics behind phishing attacks. Online webinar. https://www.cyveillance.com/web/forms/video.php?VideoID=401 (2012)
17. Daily Telegraph: "Doing a Ratner" and other famous gaffes. http://www.telegraph.co.uk/news/uknews/1573380/Doing-a-Ratner-and-other-famous-gaffes.html (2007). Accessed 22 Dec 2007
18. Deloitte: Social networking and reputational risk in the workplace—Ethics & Workplace Survey results. Deloitte LLP. http://www.slideshare.net/PingElizabeth/deloitte-2009-ethics-workplace-survey (2009)
19. Denti, L., Barbopoulos, I., Nilsson, I., Holmberg, L., Thulin, M., Wendeblad, M., Anden, L., Davidsson, E.: Sweden´s largest Facebook study. Gothenburg Research Institute Report 2012:3. http://gupea.ub.gu.se/bitstream/2077/28893/1/gupea_2077_28893_1.pdf (2012)
20. DomainTools: Domain counts & Internet statistics. http://www.whois.sc/internet-statistics/ (2013). Accessed 1 May 2013
21. Ducklin, P.: Typosquatting—what happens when you mistype a website name? Naked Secruity blog. Sophos Security. http://nakedsecurity.sophos.com/typosquatting/ (2011)
22. Eagle, L., Kitchen, P.J., Rose, L., Moyle, B.: Brand equity and brand vulnerability: the impact of gray marketing/parallel importing on brand equity and values. Eur. J. Mark. **37**(10), 1332–1349 (2003)
23. Google: Google zeitgeist 2009. http://www.google.com/intl/en/press/zeitgeist2009/ (2009)
24. Harris Interactive: 2011 Customer Experience Impact Report: getting to the heart of the consumer and brand relationship. Oracle. http://www.oracle.com/us/products/applications/cust-exp-impact-report-epss-1560493.pdf (2012)
25. Hepburn, A.: Facebook: Facts & Figures For 2010. Digital Buzz Blog. http://www.digitalbuzzblog.com/facebook-statistics-facts-figures-for-2010/ (2010). Accessed 22 March 2010
26. Hill, C.: Digital piracy: causes, consequences, and strategic response. Asia Pacific J Manage **24**(1), 9–25 (2007)
27. Hurst, N.: Angry online commenters can cause negative perceptions of corporations, MU researchers find. University of Missouri News Bureau. http://munews.missouri.edu/

news-releases/2011/0621-angry-online-commenters-can-cause-negative-perceptions-of-corporations-mu-researchers-find/ (2011). Accessed 21 June 2011
28. IFPI: Digital Music Report 2011. International Federation of the Phonographic Industry. http://www.ifpi.org/content/library/DMR2011.pdf (2011)
29. Interbrand: Best global brands 2025. Interbrand. http://interbrand.com/en/best-global-brands/previous-years/best-global-brands-2005.aspx (2005)
30. Interbrand: Best global brands 2012. Interbrand. http://interbrand.com/Libraries/Branding_Studies/Best_Global_Brands_2012.sflb.ashx?download=true (2012)
31. KarmaSnack: May 2013—Updated//Search Engine Market Share. http://www.karmasnack.com/about/search-engine-market-share/ (2013)
32. Keller, K.: Strategic brand management. Prentice Hall, New Jersey (1998)
33. Knittel, C.R., Stango, V.: "Celebrity endorsements, firm value and reputation risk: evidence from the tiger woods scandal", working paper. http://gsm.ucdavis.edu/sites/main/files/file-attachments/tiger011_web_0.pdf (2009). Accessed 1 June 2009, pp. 1–27
34. Lindemann, J.: Brand valuation : the economy of brands. Interbrand, New York (2007)
35. Mansfield-Devine, S.: Anti-social networking: exploiting the trusting environment of Web 2.0. Netw. Secur. 2008(11), 4–7 (2008)
36. Markmonitor: Brandjacking index—Online hotel bookings. https://www.markmonitor.com/download/bji/MarkMonitor_Brandjacking_Index-Spring_2011.pdf (2011)
37. Mathur, L.M.: The impact of international gray marketing on consumers and firms. J. Euromark. **4**(2), 39–59 (1995)
38. Milam, M.: The rise of brandjacking against major brands. Comput Fraud Secur. 10–13 (2008)
39. Millward Brown Optimor: Top 100 most valuable global brands 2010. Millward Brown Optimor. http://www.millwardbrown.com/Libraries/Optimor_BrandZ_Files/2010_BrandZ_Top100_Report.sflb.ashx (2010)
40. Murray, B.: Defending the brand: aggressive strategies for protecting your brand in the online arena. Amacom, New York (2004)
41. Newman, B.: The lighter side of counterfeiting puts Zippo in a fix. Wall Street Journal. http://online.wsj.com/article/SB10001424052748703362904576218650845017800.html (2011). Accessed 25 March 2011
42. Philips, C.: Free Starbucks coffee US$40 gift card Facebook scam haunts the timeline. Examiner.com. http://www.examiner.com/article/free-starbucks-coffee-40-gift-card-facebook-scam-haunts-the-timeline (2012). Accessed 1 January 2012
43. Podolny, J.: Status Signals: a sociological study of market competition. Princeton University Press, Princeton (2005)
44. Potter, H.: Needed: a systematic approach for a cockpit automation philosophy. Proceedings of Workshop on Flight Crew Accident and Incident Human Factors. 21–23 June 1995. Federal Aviation Administration, Office of System Safety. pp. A-83–84 (1995)
45. Power, R.: War & Peace in Cyberspace: don't twitter away your organisation's secrets. Comput. Fraud Secur. **8**, 18–20 (2008)
46. Prendergast, G.: Understanding consumer demand for non-deceptive pirated brands. Mark. Intel. Brands **20**(7), 405–416 (2002)
47. Remizowski, L.: GoDaddy.com founder defends elephant-hunting video. CNN.com. http://edition.cnn.com/2011/BUSINESS/04/01/godaddy.peta.protest/index.html (2011). Accessed 4 April 2011
48. Samson, T.: Spam rates hit five-year low, but phishing is on the rise. InfoWorld. http://www.infoworld.com/t/anti-spam/spam-rates-hit-five-year-low-phishing-the-rise-521 (2011). Accessed 6 June 2011
49. Schonfeld, E.: Forrester Forecast: online retail sales will grow to US$250 billion by 2014. TechCrunch. http://techcrunch.com/2010/03/08/forrester-forecast-online-retail-sales-will-grow-to-250-billion-by-2014/ (2010). Accessed 8 March 2010
50. Stumpf, S., Chaudry, P., Perretta, L.: Fake: can business stanch the flow of counterfeit products? J. Bus. Strat. **32**(2), 4–12 (2011)

51. Tagliabue, J.: scandal over poisoned wine embitters village in Austria. New York Times. http://www.nytimes.com/1985/08/02/world/scandal-over-poisoned-wine-embitters-village-in-austria.html (1985). Accessed 2 Aug 1985
52. Tamar: Transfer for US$4.99 and help save the elephants. Namecheap blog. http://community.namecheap.com/blog/2011/03/30/elephants/ (2011). Accessed 30 March 2011
53. Winter, M., Steger, U.: Managing outside pressure: strategies for preventing corporate disasters. Wiley, New York (1989)

Chapter 3
Brand Risk Management Theory

Abstract This chapter introduces a number of approaches to quantifying and communicating the nature of brand risks through, for example, the use of models and risk maps. Furthermore, it discusses a number of generic brand defence strategies that can be employed. This chapter then provides a description of typical brand risk management tools that are available commercially. However, while such tools and strategies are available, they are far from achieving ubiquity among brand owners. To understand why, this chapter presents the results of interviews with six brand owners from companies and organisations that range from small, specialist manufacturers to large multinationals. These interviews explore their perceptions of the scale of the brand risks they face, their typical methods for identifying brand risks and then their approaches to remedying any risks that have been identified. In all cases, there were no systematic methods of brand risk identification in place. Furthermore, the management strategies that were in place were often confused or weak. These interviews indicate the need for an effective brand risk management process which is straightforward to implement and maintain.

Keywords Risk model • Risk map • Online risks • Managing brand risk • Interviews • Brand risk owners

In the preceding chapter, we identified a range of different online brand risks and showed brand risks are potentially very costly both financially and reputationally. Bob Parsons's elephant video cost GoDaddy an estimated US$5 million in 1 week, the Marriott hotel in Copenhagen pays approximately US$50,000 per year in excess payments to Google, and the Domino's Pizza prank on YouTube prompted 65 % of surveyed customers to admit that they were less likely to return to Domino's in the future.

A 1997 study from Deloitte [4] concluded that the average life expectancy of a Fortune 500 company is less than 50 years and corporate risk-taking and risk-avoidance strategies could be the root cause for this. Any company's management

C. Hofman and S. Keates, *Countering Brandjacking in the Digital Age*, SpringerBriefs in Computer Science, DOI: 10.1007/978-1-4471-5580-5_3,

team has to innovate continuously to ensure that the company will continue to thrive. In this process of innovation, the risk scenarios will change and evolve. Too much risk aversion and a company will stagnate and then inevitably be overtaken by competitors. Too much risk taking and a company may gamble too heavily on a strategy that fails, leaving the company with insufficient assets or credit to continue trading. The usual consequences of failed gambles of this type are take-over by a competitor or winding up the business. Failure to adequately protect the brands owned by a company is an unnecessary risk to take and one that also carries potentially catastrophic consequences. Again, the Ratner story is the obvious example. So, companies who want to genuinely manage their risk profile have to be aware of where their brand is exposed and how to manage it.

The principal objective with brand risk management is to proactively avoid potential brand risks and eliminate or contain existing brand risks, all with the express intention of ensuring that overall brand value is not being diminished.

Abrahams identifies four fields of brand risk and its management ([1], p. 33):

1. Delivery: The brand needs to deliver consistently.
2. Renewal: The brand has to renew its promise.
3. Protection: The brand has to build goodwill via a protection strategy.
4. Response: The brand has to be able to respond if there is an imminent catastrophe scenario.

To sum up, good brand risk management is not only about putting out fires, but is also to build a long-term prevention plan.

Copulsky states that an efficient brand risk management system has to make everyone understand what brand value is, what drives it and thus, by extension, what could threaten it. A brand risk management policy has to be communicated effectively and employees should feel valued for their contribution ([3], p. 93). The whole system should lay the foundation for collective learning, so employees are able to share information freely.

Copulsky's 7-step model for managing brand risk shown in Fig. 3.1 suggests, how companies should manage brand risk [3].

Let us now examine the different steps:

Step 1—Assess brand risks

A brand owner can assess possible brand risks via a risk map, i.e. a matrix on which all the known brand risks are placed. See Fig. 3.2 for an example. The mapping will show which brand risks are the most important ones to be aware of. The horizontal axis shows likeliness of the brand risk and the vertical axis shows the financial impact that the brand risk will have. For convenience the risk map can be divided into range intervals (priority 1–4). For instance, the brand risk leading to Domino's Pizza's YouTube video would rank in the Priority 1 field.

The estimated impact should both include direct and indirect consequences. It is possible that various low risk events taken together can have a high impact. When mapping risks it is important to consider if the brand owner can control the potential risk factor. For example, cybersquatting can be avoided by having an

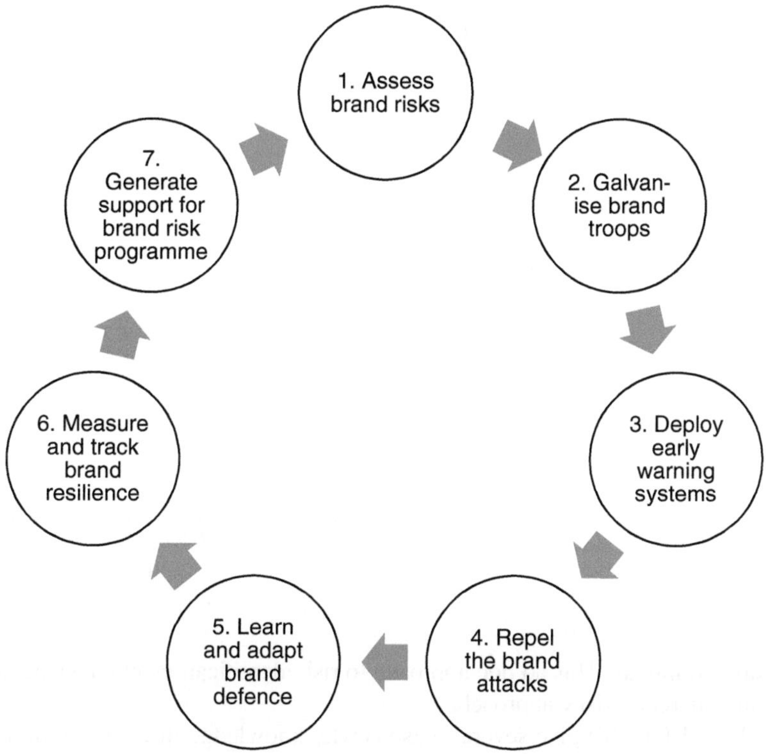

Fig. 3.1 Copulsky's seven-step model for managing brand risk and recovery [3]

active domain name strategy. On the other hand, sudden changes in legislation or Internet practices are far more difficult to influence proactively.

Step 2—Galvanize brand troops

Copulsky's experience is that brand risk management is traditionally no single person's job. "Reputation" is typically managed by a company's Public Relations Department, while "brand licensing" is often the responsibility of the Legal Department. Even these are only parts of brand risk management. Most other protection seems to be reactive ([3], p. 49). Weber [9] argues that organizations are still structured as in the 1960s in terms of their view of management of brands. As a consequence, adjusting to something new, such as developing a social media strategy, often requires cooperative and coordinated action by several departments within a company. This dislocation of responsibility means there is often no clear chain of command or even clear courses of action. Who is responsible for identifying a brand risk? Who do they inform? Who has ownership of addressing the issue? All of these questions become more difficult to answer when the responsibility is distributed across multiple parts of a company. In the absence of a confirmed brand risk strategy that spells out roles and responsibilities across the whole organisation, companies are often left relying on the diligence of individual employees identifying and

Fig. 3.2 The brand risk map

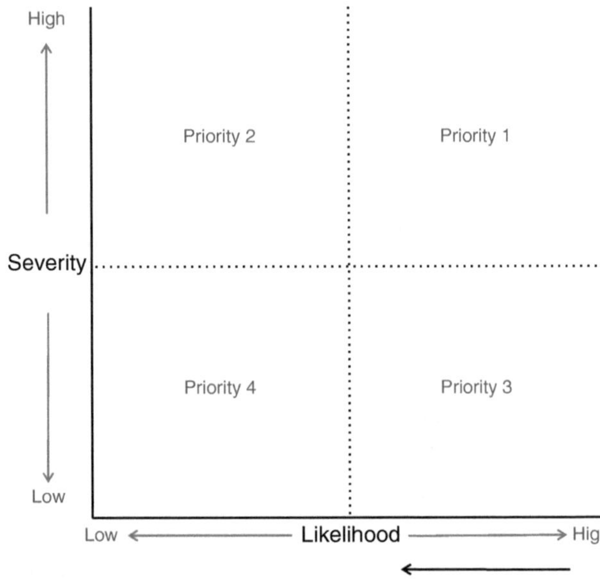

responding to threats. This ad hoc approach to risk identification and management is clearly an inherently risky approach.

Schulz and Jobe [8] give several reasons why knowledge flows are important in organizations:

1. They transmit knowledge across the organization.
2. They facilitate the coordination of workflows.
3. They can enable organizations to capitalize on business opportunities requiring the collaboration of several sub-units.
4. They can help execute a unified strategic response to moves by competitors, customers and suppliers.
5. They enable the recognition and exploitation of economies of scale and scope.

Managing brand risk is likely to continue to be spread out in organizations today. Typically, Legal Departments will continue to register trademarks, IT Departments will manage domain names registrations and Marketing will be responsible for branding and social media, etc. This distribution of responsibility is simply recognising that brand protection requires different technical skills to address different parts of the overall strategy. Lawyers need to do the legal stuff and IT experts need to administer the online web presence. The consequence of this, though, is that it is essential that companies have very clear strategies for coordinating the activities of brand protection across all the relevant departments. As regards the "chain of command", the most effective solution is to appoint a board-level champion explicitly charged with overall responsibility for management of brand risk.

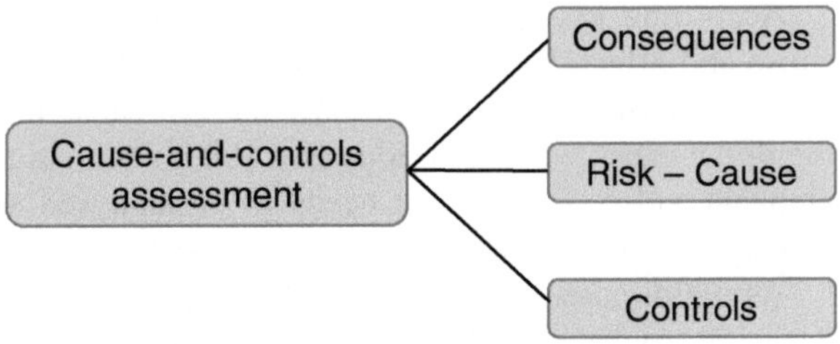

Fig. 3.3 Cause-and-controls assessment [1]

Step 3—Deploy early warning systems

The ability to react swiftly to brand risks once they have been identified is a key factor in good brand risk management. Conversely, not reacting to an abuse of a trademark can lead to that trademark being considered generic. Forgetting to register a domain name when launching a new brand can be costly in legal fees when it subsequently has to be recovered through legal action. Not closing down a counterfeiting site or an unauthorized grey market outlet will lead to direct loss of turnover from the brand and—especially for premium brands—have a long term damaging effect on its overall reputation for exclusivity. A brand owner needs, therefore, to have an early warning system in place. In Step 2, we discussed the importance of educating employees about brand risks so they will be aware of any if they see them. Additionally, the company has to organize the associated information flows so any brand risks will he handled correctly. The use of different tools to detect brand risk is possible as well and we will return to this issue in a later chapter.

Step 4—Repel the brand attacks

In Step 1, brand risks were identified and prioritized. Step 2 explained how companies should educate their employees. Step 3 argues why it is important to react swiftly to any perceived threats. Step 4 addresses how to react in practice to a particular identified brand risk. When a brand risk is discovered, it is important to know how to react to this threat, and take action, so the brand risk will be eliminated or contained. For example, a cybersquatting site can be taken down through legal means. A grey market importer can be ordered to comply with the brand requirements in that market, and so on. The important point here is to have known responses in place ready to use as soon as the threat is detected.

Step 5—Learn and adapt brand defence

It is imperative that, as organisations learn more about the nature of the brand threats that they face, they also learn to adapt and modify their brand defence strategies to minimise the risk posed by those threats. A "learning" organisation will have the ability to prevent future brand risks, when it develops the capacity to learn its experiences. However, to do so, a framework is needed for classifying and analysing the origins of risk and the potential consequences of that risk. Methods of control for managing the risk can then be developed. The cause-and-controls assessment model shown in Fig. 3.3 provides such a framework.

According to Abrahams it is important, yet difficult, to distinguish between cause and effect. When a risk event occurs, there is a direct cause, also called the efficient cause. It is, however, only the last cause in a long chain. As an example, the direct cause when GoDaddy lost 100,000 domains in 1 week was Bob Parsons' elephant video. Each cause needs to be analysed separately. The main cause is usually heavily rooted in the culture of the particular organization.

As we discussed earlier, the risk mapping of the impact of a brand risk events can vary. As each brand is different from another in context, character and condition, there are just too many combinations to hypothesize about the effects on brand value over time when suffering risk events. In the case of Domino's Pizza, there is a general opinion that Domino's reacted quickly to limit damages and the losses were consequently not as severe as they might have been, if their response had been slower. However, the impact of brand risk events is cumulative. Even if a single event has been handled successfully, any subsequent event will require even greater corrective effort, because customers may then remember the preceding event and begin to reconsider whether the company may, after all, not be completely blameless. Thus, it becomes ever harder to manage brand risk if a series of risk events is permitted to occur.

New brand risks are occurring all the time. Consequently, it is essential for organizations to learn and adapt in the process. According to Knud Illeriis, learning is

> ...fundamentally an integrated process, which consists of two sub-processes, which interact: The individual and its surroundings via direct contact or though different media. Secondly, the inner self's working and adaptation process of learning... [5].

The individual learning process can be illustrated by Kolb's model shown in Fig. 3.4.

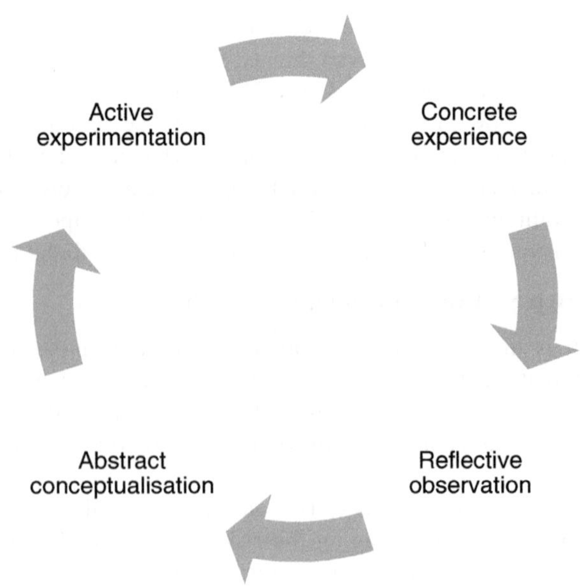

Fig. 3.4 Kolb's four stages for individual learning [6]

Kolb's model expresses that learning is a continual process that is based on acquired experience. For example, consider a lawyer in a Legal Department in a company who discovers that someone has registered a domain name which is very similar to a trademark that the company owns (concrete experience). The lawyer then considers what can be done based on what has been learnt already (reflective observation) and concludes that there are two different solutions after analysing the situation: (1) the company can buy the domain name from the registrant or (2) the company can pursue the registrant legally (abstract conceptualization). In the end the lawyer decides to go for the second solution (active experimentation). How did it go? Was it successful or not? What was learnt that can benefit the organization the next time a similar event happens (concrete experience)? What is good about Kolb's model is that it shows that abstract thinking and observation is not only sufficient to learn, you also have to experiment and act.

Argyris and Schön [2] distinguish between single loop and double loop learning. Single loop learning is about correcting a simple error, without questioning the complete framework of the company's brand risk management. This could, for instance, be a correction of which department should handle a specific brand risk task or improving a process to fix a brand risk. Double loop learning is discovering an error and questioning the model. If we take the single loop examples, then the questions to answer would be, why did the brand risk problem end up in the wrong department, and why was the process not efficient?

Step 6—Measure and track brand resilience

The brand owner needs to measure the performance of the brand risk control mechanisms, both as a motivator to see what has been done, but also for when they need to "sell" the brand risk program inside the organisation. Copulsky separates brand risk measuring and tracking into three levels ([3], p. 171):

Level 1: Emerging

The Marketing Department collects regularly customer data through surveys and conversation, but the data collection is ad hoc and there is no systematic tracking.

Level 2: Developing

The collection of customer data is regularized with standardized measurements. The company's top management is getting involved and there is greater awareness of potential brand risks.

Level 3: Cutting edge

The regular collection of customer data as in level 2, is supplemented by on-going reporting regarding the brand value. Executives are viewed as brand officers and brand risk management is part of an overall risk management program.

Step 7—Generate support for brand risk program

The measurement results—if positive—should be used to generate general support in the organisation, to ensure that management is continuously focused on integrating brand risk management on the Internet, and ensure that employees are aware of the importance of the brand and brand value.

3.1 Existing Brand Risk Management Tools

There are different brand risk management tools in the market today. In this section, we will examine two total solutions, which comprise both brand risk monitoring and management.

CPA Global offers a tool that allows the monitoring of general observations on the Internet and on auction sites in particular. It also offers a series of enforcement options. The user navigates between these features via a series of on-screen tabs.

The Internet section lists infringing domain names, web content containing a specified brand name, changes to suspect websites or registrants, and sponsored links. The user can uncheck boxes if they wish to filter results according to type of threat, date or who the task has been assigned to. The auction section lists potential counterfeit products on Internet auction sites.

Once a possible risk has been detected and identified, the brand risk manager can send an e-mail to the infringing party through CPA's service. There are different templates to choose between, depending of the nature of the suspected infringement and thus the warning e-mail required.

The Enforcement tab also records the history of the potential infringement cases. The brand risk manager can see the status of each case, the person assigned to each case and also any activity in each case. The purpose is to help the brand risk manager to stay up to date with the developments in all cases and check the details of the each infringement. The manager can also set the system to provide regular status reports direct to their inbox.

CitizenHawk offers similar monitoring functions. However, they are also focussed on showing results from the brand risk eliminations. According to a representative from NightHawk, numbers are essential to convince customers that online brand protection works. They use an estimator bot value to show how much the customer has earned by protecting their brand.

Their Estibot makes a calculation based on the conversion rate for recovered web traffic. By knowing the brand's conversion rate per 1,000 visitors, and the value of a customer's first order they can show the dollar amount that the brand owner has earned by this brand risk management. The calculation is similar to that shown in the Appendix of this book for Norwegian Air Shuttle.

Schandelbauer confirms that one of the big challenges is how to break down the enormous amount of raw data in a way that makes sense to the brand owner. One way is to use colour coding to categorize the brand risk importance.

Both systems are based on spreadsheets. While CPA is more like an organised structure to the brand risk manager's alternative spreadsheet, the NightHawk tool sorts through the raw data and come up with solutions. Both solutions use visual aids in form of screenshots of websites and product photos. This is very helpful to scan quickly. NightHawk's use of colour coding is another way to grasp the important areas.

3.2 Expected Adoption Patterns for Brand Risk Management Processes

Brand owners whose customers are on the Internet are the most "lowest hanging fruit" in this context. Their brands are most at risk from social media activity, for example. Consequently, such brand owners should be looking very seriously at adopting a brand risk management process and especially one that addresses online and social media risks explicitly. However, the reality is that not everyone adopts innovative products and processes immediately. There is a known pattern of adoption followed by different types of adopters.

Geoffrey Moore's model, "The technology adoption life cycle", is useful when it comes to identify the adoption patterns of a new product, service or process [7]. In his model, the adopters are divided into five categories: Innovators, Early adopters, Early majority, Late majority and Laggards.

The Innovators are the first movers. They are the ones standing in line to get a new Apple product on its launch day. While the Innovators buy into something because it is new, the Early Adopters will buy into it because of the benefit of the new technology, or new process in this case. They do not need the same well-established references as the Early Majority. The Late Majority needs the same proven references as the Early Majority, however, they are not as comfortable with technology as the Early Majority, and the need to be able to trust the new product is really important. The Laggards will probably never embrace any new process until very late in its life.

As for how mature the demand for brand risk management processes is, which is itself an indicator of overall level of awareness of the issues, it is worth looking at the customers of brand risk management companies, such as the European Domain Centre (EDC). Their clients are mostly based in the Early Majority segment. They are the type of adopters who need to make sure that it works before they buy into it. The clients are usually larger companies with an internal Legal Department, or a department that is responsible for domain names. They are typically comfortable with the Internet and are confident that web services can solve the practical challenges that they face today. Some clients will have experience managing their own domain names for years now. The reason for choosing a company such as EDC in the first place is principally the convenience offered, for example that all top level domains can be registered in one place.

With the client profile of such companies showing an emphasis towards the Early Majority type adopters, this suggests that the prevalence of awareness of the risks and appetite or ability to address those risks is not as universal as might be expected. To explore this further, we conducted a series of interviews with brand risk owners to find their level of awareness of the risks and their overall level of preparedness for managing them.

3.3 Interviews with Brand Risk Owners

Interviews were conducted with six European companies, all of whom were owners of well-known brands. For the purposes of anonymity, these shall be referred to by their generic field of operation, specifically: ChemicalCom; AudioCom; CloudCom; GamblingCom; TransportCom; and, EnergyCom. Please note here that any reference to any existing company with these names is entirely coincidental. These names have been chosen to simply be indicators of their field of operation and not the actual names of the companies.

The people interviewed were all involved in some form of brand risk management, especially in the area of trademarks and domain names. Brand risk is a confidential area for many companies and so interviews were conducted to get the necessary information. It was not clear how companies organize responsibility for brand risk management internally. Consequently, it was decided to use the Legal Departments as a starting point and then contact other employees in the organisation if they were also involved in brand protection. All interviews were held at the respective company premises and were recorded then later transcribed. The interviews usually took 1 h. Apart from the first two interviews with Chemical and Audio, the Risk Map described by Copulsky [3] was used to assist the conversation. The interviewees were asked to physically place different brand risks on the risk map and explain their reasons for doing so. This helped provide additional valuable information that was potentially withheld during in the first two interviews. Legal Departments are known to be of a careful nature, so the use of the Risk Maps helped make them more open about their experiences with brand risk. The interviews focused on the risks to the principal brands especially, i.e. the single brand, or collection of brands in some instances, for which the companies concerned were most famous. In some cases, although not all, the principal brand shared the same name as the brand owning company. This was more typical for the smaller companies. The larger companies owned multiple brands of varying levels of importance to them.

3.3.1 ChemicalCom

ChemicalCom is headquartered in a European capital city and was recently acquired by a multinational company for over US$5 billion. With more than 80 offices globally, ChemicalCom is a world leader in two areas:

1. Food ingredients: supplying leading food manufacturers worldwide with bio-based food ingredients like emulsifiers, cultures, natural sweeteners and gums.
2. Industrial enzymes: supplying enzymes to industries such as animal nutrition, detergents, bioethanol, textile treatment, carbohydrate processing and food and beverages.

So ChemicalCom's brand is not on the shelves, but is well known in the business-to-business area. Tom is the Trade Mark Manager responsible for registration and management of trademarks, domain names and other rights such as contract details. His department consists of four members. They work closely with the marketing team and product managers when new brand names are suggested. His function is to verify that new brand names do not conflict with existing brands and test if the brand has uniqueness to be registered as a trademark. It is of course preferable that a brand name can be protected as a trademark. However, if a great name cannot be protected legally, they will use it anyway. They do a trademark check and, eventually, a domain name check to test availability. It takes usually some days to investigate. Domain names and trademarks are registered directly with the registry. ChemicalCom has more than 4,000 trademarks and hundreds of brands.

Furthermore, they monitor if there are infringing trademark applications that are too close to their intellectual property. These reports are prepared by an external consulting company. Brand infringements are usually discovered by different people in the organization, who will then contact the Legal Department by e-mail. It is usually from someone close to the market in the Sales or Marketing Departments. Tom will then evaluate the legal proceedings. Cases are usually resolved before they end in court. If there is no response to written warnings, he calls on ChemicalCom's large local network to contact the infringer. ChemicalCom is not an obvious case for counterfeiting, given that their products are not directly consumer related, but he does not exclude out the possibility. During the interview, Tom was shown an example of Chinese manufacturers offering a trademarked product from ChemicalCom.

Tom said that these kinds of cases are taken very seriously if the brand is distinctive for ChemicalCom and if the trademark is also protected in the infringing country. The product in the example shown to Tom was only protected in the European Union and thus beyond ChemicalCom's control. ChemicalCom hosts and manages all their domain names themselves. Tom felt that it was time to clean up the catalogue of domain names held, as there are many that they were not using anymore.

3.3.2 AudioCom

AudioCom is a global leader in headset solutions. The headsets are promoted solely under their principal brand name and they cater both to the office market and the private consumer market. They employ 900 people with various local sales offices worldwide. AudioCom is owned by a larger parent company. The total parent group's turnover was US$1 billion in 2010, of which AudioCom generated US$300 million.

Karl is the VP of Intellectual Property Rights at AudioCom. His department consists of four people specializing in trademarks, domain names, patents and other intellectual rights. They currently administer 200–300 international trademarks registered in 60 countries. They work directly with Marketing to ensure that their principal brand is consistently protected. Marketing have them examine the distinctiveness of possible sub-brands to be protected as trademarks. Karl's department will either use an internal search tool or have the Trademark Department assist. If their recommendation is positive, they will get the go ahead to register it as a trademark. This task is handled by e-mail between the two departments. They have quarterly meetings where they evaluate the current procedures and any other IP related issue. Toni from the Trademark Department registers the domain names and informs the IT Department when registered, so they can take care of the technical issues. Both Toni and the IT Department have access to the administration panel of their external domain registrar company.

All domains are in general pointed to the website of their principal brand. Partner companies, usually distributors, do sometimes register local domains, such as *.it* and *.hu*, which name the principal brand explicitly. This is usually a consequence of internal confusion, as AudioCom should be the owners of any domain name where possible. Every 6 months an audit report is generated by the external domain registrar company, which is used together with information from Marketing to evaluate whether certain domains should be discontinued. They have currently 600 domains and wish to keep it limited, because it is quite costly to maintain and protect all of those domains.

They have experienced cybersquatting of the principal brand name and they have had to take legal action to get back the *.hu*-registered domain from an old distributor. They had a similar case with a *.it*-registered domain, where they did not manage to recover the domain due to a lack of evidence of bad faith from the registrant's side.

Karl is satisfied with the current administrative system to handle their IP documents, but he does admit that the IT platform could be better. With the volume of IP rights to manage and trademarks to renew periodically they do spend a lot of time on handling this.

Regarding paid placement, they have contacted Google to ensure that no one else advertises for their trademark as search term on Adwords. They get around ten requests per month from business partners, which are approved after confirmation from the local country manager. Toni is contacting Google to allow these partners to use their trademark. There was evidence of competitors using their registered principal brand as part of a search term to point to non-approved resellers.

The Marketing Department is responsible for their Facebook page. Karl confirmed that he was the one who initially informed Marketing to register the principal brand name on the social networks as a social media username. They do not own the corresponding profiles on other networks such as Twitter and YouTube, though.

Counterfeiting of their headsets does exist, however, Karl does not feel that it is a serious threat. They used to monitor eBay, however, the task was overwhelming. Their focus is now to stop predominantly Chinese counterfeit manufacturers more directly instead, through the use of detectives. It is still difficult as that there is a whole network of companies working together, who tip each other off and do not keep much stock. Regarding grey markets, they do sell surplus stock via dealers in markets where they are not operating, such as in South America. Another secondary market exists for defect products, which are repaired and resold. They consider it a good branding move in new markets, though they do admit that there are occasional channel conflicts. Internal communication has vastly improved in general, but more could be done to get information about brand risk spread out in the organisation.

3.3.3 CloudCom

CloudCom's service enables customers to receive documents containing sensitive information, such as bank statements, pay slips, invoices, public notifications and the like, in a personal and secure online archive. Established in 2001, the company's mission has been to digitize the delivery of documents that customers would usually receive by mail. 2.3 million people and 127,000 companies used the CloudCom solution in 2010. CloudCom is a comparatively small organisation with 17 employees. Turnover was US$13 million in 2010.

Ernie is the product and development director at CloudCom. Building on his former career in the domain name industry, he is also responsible for trademarks and domain names. Trademarks and other legal issues such as any type of infringement is handled by their lawyers

Their domain names used to be spread out with different domain registrars, but after streamlining the process they are now only using one registrar. Ernie decides which domains to register and either does it himself via the domain registrar's admin portal or by e-mailing the account manager at the domain registrar. The domain portfolio is fairly small and they have a clear strategy over which domains to go after. Due to the generic nature of their three principal brand names, it has been difficult for them to claim rights to previously registered domains. In these cases, they have purchased those domains instead if necessary. There is no standard monitoring of domain names in place, so domain infringements are discovered randomly. They do dispute the serious infringements. For instance one of their partners discovered that a French company marketed a similar service under a very similar name. Their lawyers send them a report each time a potentially infringing trademark is applied for. There is a high level of direct browser traffic especially from the local domains, so different variations are valuable and have to be registered.

Their Marketing Department monitors what is said about the brand on the social networks. They receive a daily report about CloudCom mentions. The service is mainly used for marketing, however, Ernie does see possibilities to use the tool to check for negative stories as well.

In the Risk Map shown in Fig. 3.5, Ernie placed social media usernames as high risk, given that they had not yet secured these names on other social networks than Facebook. Their social network strategy is still being evaluated. Marketing is responsible for this project, however Ernie is also involved. They already have 17,000 fans on Facebook, but as he states *we are still not world champions*. He feels that the impact can be quite high if they do not manage to get their names.

Fig. 3.5 CloudCom Risk Map according to Ernie

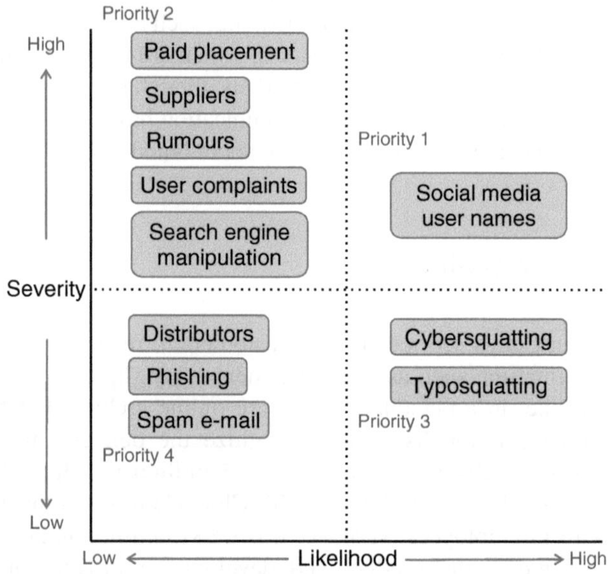

He listed several other threats as Priority 2 risks. None of these were being monitored systematically.

Given that the brand has such a high level of awareness, they do get their share of user complaints. It does regulate itself, as other customers will then defend CloudCom. As CloudCom are closely linked to another similar system, he does see that this relation can affect them especially when there are rumours of security lacks at the other company.

3.3.4 GamblingCom

GamblingCom is the monopolistic betting and gaming company in its home country. Partly owned by the state (80 %) and by other sports clubs and associations (20 %), they had a turnover in 2010 of US$1.8 billion.

Melanie is the in-house lawyer at GamblingCom. Together with her colleague in the Legal Department, she handles any legal issue ranging from intellectual property rights to any form of contracts and game rules. Intellectual property issues such as infringements of immaterial rights and registrations of trademarks and domains take up 10–20 % of her time. The workload is usually heaviest when a new game launches. Choosing a brand name starts at Marketing or the Product Departments, which will come up with suggestions for a name. She will then verify its distinctiveness and the more unique the name, the easier it will be to protect. According to Melanie, there is a continuous battle with Marketing about ensuring that brand name suggestions are not generic. In her opinion, there is still no streamlined procedure regarding product launches.

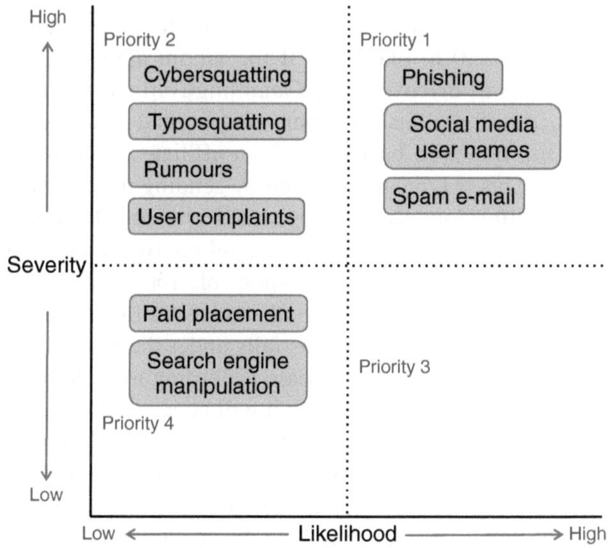

Fig. 3.6 GamblingCom Risk Map according to Melanie

When a brand name is approved, they will apply for the corresponding domestic trademark and the relevant domain names. Melanie will send an e-mail to the Online Marketing Department and they decide which domain names to register.

Timothy from the Online Marketing Department confirmed that they register the generic domains *.com*, *.net* and *.org*, *.eu* and the local domestic domains. They also register the most expected typographical error variations of those names to allow for users misspelling or mistyping the URLs. Secondly, they receive weekly reports from their external domain registrar company on whether there are any domain registrations in their name. The GamblingCom trademarks are registered via a trademark agency, which also sends them reports, if there are domestic or EU applications infringing on their brands. Regarding domains they are trying to be more proactive, after several domain disputes in the past. Online gambling is big business, so they have to be continually alert to this risk.

They are usually informed about infringements from the Customer Service Department and sometimes by other departments and any of the regional managers. Any infringing party will usually then receive a warning letter, although it depends on the seriousness of the case. The Legal Department has a general budget for any IP protection issue, but there is no fixed economic limit. Melanie did emphasize, though, that there was no budget allowance for an extra employee in her section and so their monitoring activities cannot be expensive. Melanie placed the different online brand threats in the Risk Map shown in Fig. 3.6.

Melanie placed three online brand threats in the Priority 1 box. Phishing was considered a highly likely risk given that they are a well-known brand. They have only had very few cases to date, but the risk is expected to escalate with the liberalization with an anticipated increase in the potential market. She comments that it is difficult to go after companies offering illegal games situated in other jurisdictions, as they do not appear in the domestic courts. Just recently, they had a case of e-mail spam, where the victim was directed to GamblingCom's free games and offered US$30 to play with if the victim agreed to reveal certain personal data. The case was discovered by GamblingCom's Customer Service Department when the victim complained to them that he had not received this money. Most cases of spam, however, have been from affiliates, who had not read the contract thoroughly. This is typically stopped by sending them a warning letter.

GamblingCom has not registered any social media usernames yet apart from on Facebook. There has been general confusion between the Marketing and Legal Departments over who was responsible for such registrations. On the one hand, it is brand protection and thus falls under the Legal Department, on the other hand it is a social media task and thus falls under the Marketing Department. She adds that it is not a classic protection case according to trademark law, However, if someone takes their Twitter profile, then it will be a case for the Legal Department to resolve. Their usernames are already taken on Twitter and YouTube by third parties.

In the Priority 2 box, she placed "domain names". GamblingCom has become more aware of the importance of brand protection, however there are still cases of cybersquatting that they have to challenge. They are currently disputing some infringing domain cases such as *.com* and *.net* registrations of their principal brand name, which were registered before their current policy. To see how their domain policy worked, an availability check of the domain names of the latest trademark registrations was performed of the collection of the seven most important trademarks owned by GamblingCom against *.com*, *.eu*, *.net*, *.org* and domestic domains. Of the 35 possible combinations of the 7 brand names and 5 domains, only 14 were registered and 21 were unregistered.

Some trademarks were not registered as domain names at all and there was not a consistent registration of top-level domains across the full range of trademarks. Some trademarks were registered for some domains, while others were registered to a different collection of domains. Perhaps to help explain this inconsistency, it is worth noting that GamblingCom had used different external domain registrars and registrant data for a number of the trademarks.

GamblingCom does take user complaints very seriously, primarily to ensure customer satisfaction. However, they also recognise that their status as a high profile, state owned company means that they have a greater obligation to handle such cases correctly. They feel that they tend to compensate too many players if there are suspicions of internal errors in their games to avoid any potentially negative public relations.

Melanie placed paid placement and search engine manipulation low in the Risk Map. However, that does not mean that there is not someone abusing their brand, it just means that the brand risk cost is not considered high.

3.3.5 TransportCom

TransportCom is a small specialist company that manufactures three-wheeled cargo cycles primarily used for the transportation of children around cities. Its main customer base is urban families. The owner and founder of the company, Neil, made the original prototype in 1999 and got such a great response that he quit his day job to start production on a full-time basis. With an annual turnover of US$3 million, 10 employees and 7,000 bikes on the streets, they have managed to carve a niche where the TransportCom brand has a high level of customer awareness. They have started exporting and another overseas company manufactures the tricycle under licence for retail in two other countries. They have seven different cycle types under the TransportCom brand, which is registered as a European trademark. Their flagship store and manufacturing is situated in a European capital city. Additionally, they market the TransportCom brand via their website and through word of mouth from satisfied customers.

Figure 3.7 shows the Risk Map of TransportCom according to Neil.

Neil placed social media usernames as the only Priority 1 risk. The company is present on Facebook and LinkedIn, however, they are not using TransportCom, which is also the company's principal brand, as the address. Furthermore, TransportCom is already registered to third parties on sites such as YouTube and Twitter.

Regarding paid placements on search engines, there have been examples of competitors paying to appear in the results for searches on TransportCom's trademarks. Once in a while, Neil does some Google searches, but it is not a routine assignment. If he finds evidence of such behaviour by a competitor, he sends the competitor a warning to remove the advertisement. That will normally work. He is not aware that a filter can be created at Google so that rival companies will not appear in the results for searches using his brand name.

There were no competitors appearing directly in search results solely for TransportCom in Google. However, they do appear for combinations of search terms that include TransportCom, such as "TransportCom cycles."

Fig. 3.7 TransportCom Risk Map according to Neil

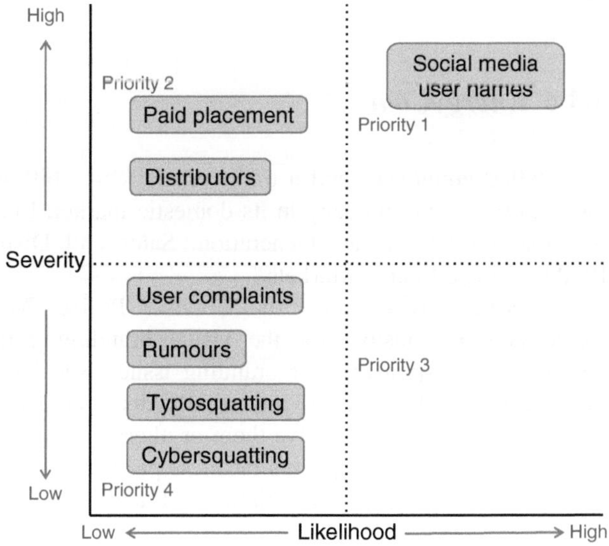

90 % of TransportCom's distributors, which are bicycle stores, also sell competing brands. Given that distributor profits are lower than for TransportCom's most direct competitor, Neil is aware that the stores are more likely to promote the competition's products

He placed a couple of other brand threats as Priority 4. He says that it is unavoidable that there are unhappy customers. However, there was only one negative comment on Facebook, although that result is ranked high in Google results when doing a search for TransportCom, which annoys him. He feels that the complaint is out of proportion. He prefers to let happy customers defend the brand instead of replying.

At one point, TransportCom had a production error and they sent out warning letters to all customers as soon as the problem came to light. It was also addressed on their website. Neil believes that a quick, public response gives trustworthiness and maintains loyal customers.

They have registered the domain names for TransportCom in the countries where they are present. In some countries, their local agent has registered the domain name, but this can lead to difficulties. TransportCom does have a legal dispute with their German ex-partner, who is not willing to hand over the domain. Neil is not overly worried about others registering domains using his trademark. A bike shop has registered TransportComCycles, but Neil does not believe that it will give the registrant any valuable traffic. When researching his domain portfolio, they are only the owner of *TransportCom.com* and the domestic TransportCom domain. The remaining domain name variants are owned by agents.

In general, Neil does not feel that these brand risk are serious threats to his business. What matters to him is a great product and service. His existing customers are great sales ambassadors, so their focus is on producing quality bikes and relying on their reputation for quality. His greatest fear is the day that a similar quality bike will be launched.

3.3.6 EnergyCom

With 6,000 employees and a turnover of US$12 billion in 2010, EnergyCom is the largest energy company in its domestic market. EnergyCom is set up as four principal business areas: Generation, Sales and Distribution, Exploration and Production and Energy Markets.

Katherine was formerly the Creative Project Manager in the Marketing Department responsible for the visual branding guidelines. Given her internal status as responsible for branding issues, she has dealt with several brand infringements. These issues are usually discovered by her colleagues, and she then evaluates if she can solve them or alternatively hand them over to the Legal Department. She also approves business partners' use of the EnergyCom logo on their website. Her personal attitude to branding guides her decisions regarding brand risk. While they have a visual brand manual, they do not have a brand risk manual, so each case is treated on its own merits. Regarding business partners' use of their logo, it will only be allowed if it is a win/win situation for both parties. She recognizes that there is no systematic monitoring of who is using the logo, however, the organization has many watchdogs. Katherine's Risk Map is shown in Fig. 3.8.

Katherine placed Rumours as the most serious Priority 1 online brand risk. EnergyCom is very cautious about, and protective of, its public profile. Being state-owned, and a dominant player in the energy industry, puts them in a prominent position in the public consciousness. They have a Public Relations Department, which handles any case that could affect the EnergyCom brand adversely, such as if it ends up in the press. She mentioned, for instance, a mining accident in South America at an EnergyCom supplier, where they chose to take immediate action and went to visit the site of the accident to show that they were treating the incident seriously.

User complaints were placed as Priority 2 given that they are closely linked to rumours. When Katherine started in the company, her manager told her to ignore angry user complaints on the Internet. They should only react to the bigger issues. Social media usernames were placed as Priority 3. At the time of writing this, they had run a campaign on Facebook, but were awaiting further guidelines from Management. She is not too worried about names already taken, as she states that they can surely recover them. She feels, however, that being slow to react is a signal to external lookers-on that EnergyCom is not seen as a company on the cutting edge and consequently such perceived sluggishness is bad for branding.

Bernard is the Digital Manager at EnergyCom. His department of 12 employees handles the content on the customer website. 70 % of all sales in the organisation go through them. He confirms that they are awaiting the decision regarding

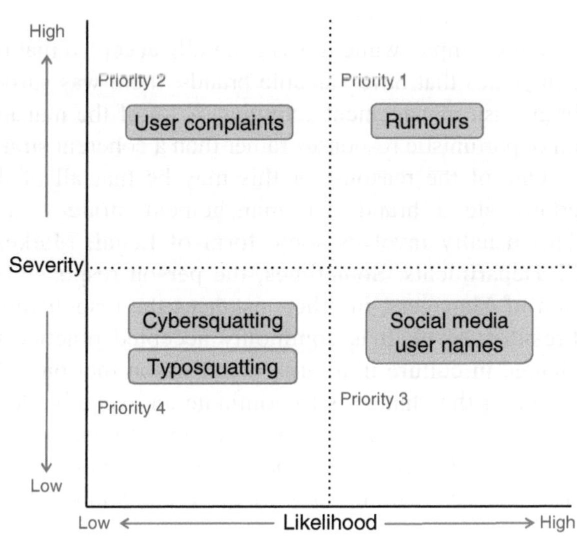

Fig. 3.8 EnergyCom Risk map according to Katherine

the strategic approach to social media, but he feels that they are far too cautious. He does place social media usernames as a higher risk priority than Katherine. A quick Internet search showed that their principal brand name was taken on Twitter and YouTube by third parties.

They have 600 domain names. Some years ago, they underwent a process of rationalisation and cleaned up their catalogue, but there is still no consistent domain name policy in place. Bernard is aware that misspelled and mistyped variations of the domain names are relevant, as he has seen the level of traffic they generate. It is usually the Legal Department that informs them when a new trademark has been registered by EnergyCom and they will then register the domain names in Digital Marketing. Sometimes their media bureau is involved as well with recommendations. Further Internet searches showed that domain registrations are not consistent, with nineteen out of a possible 28 domains registered for the two main variations of the principal brand name.

In one instance, they had submitted trademark applications without registering the corresponding domain names and the .com domain name was registered by a third party in the time between the public announcement and the registration of the domain names by EnergyCom. This example illustrates the need for a coordinated company-wide strategy to brand protection and brand risk management. This was a cybersquat that was clearly preventable with a more holistic internal approach to managing the risk.

3.4 Findings from the Brand Owner Interviews

The interviews gave insight into how companies structure brand risk management today and how they view the threat level of different known brand risks. A few generalizable trends can be seen.

For example, while it was generally accepted that brand risk is a major issue for companies that have valuable brands, there was surprisingly little structure to the brand risk management activities. A lot of the management appeared to be based on opportunistic responses rather than a coherent strategy.

One of the reasons for this may be that all of the large companies have to coordinate a brand risk management strategy across multiple departments. This usually involves some form of Legal, Marketing, Customer Service and IT Departments. Sometimes, the person responsible was a Manager or collection of Managers, in other instances the responsibility went up as high as Vice President level. It is commonly accepted practice that when trying to instil a change in culture in a large organisation that one of the most effective ways of effecting the change is to nominate an executive level champion of the change. The comparative absence of such champions on all but one of the companies interviewed suggests that brand risk management is still not seen as a high priority activity within many of these companies. The example from EnergyCom of a new brand being announced 2 months before the relevant domains were registered is an excellent example of the damaging disconnects that can happen between departments when there is not singular voice coordinating such activities and with an overall view and ownership of the whole brand risk management strategy.

There was also very little evidence of systematic monitoring of potential threats. Where monitoring took place, it appeared to be largely by chance (where someone stumbled across a cybersquat or similar) or conducted by external companies, usually the domain registrar. Even then, the monitoring tended to be based on trademark infringement rather than brand risk per se. Given that early identification of brand risks is essential to any effective brand risk management strategy, the lack of systematic monitoring is a major omission. Risk management strategies cannot begin to take effect if the risk is not known about.

Most companies were aware of the importance of search engine results, but again there was little evidence of systematic monitoring or management of such results for their principal brand names. This is potentially a very major omission, as this offers a very effective route for competitors to divert business away from the brand owner. There is a clear need for the brand owners to address this issue.

Almost all of the companies had either experienced cybersquatting or were worried about it. However, again it was rare to find a coherent and coordinated approach to managing this. In several instances, the registration process of domain names was inconsistently followed, so it is not very surprising that potential cybersquat domains were left unregistered. It is clear that companies need to develop more sophisticated and effective methods of identifying all of the potential domain names, including likely misspellings and mistypings, and registering them consistently. A common problem appeared to be distributors and partners registering local domains for the principal brands. This is potentially of little consequence where the partnerships are solid. However, these can become highly problematic when the partnerships break down. Brand owners would be well advised to ensure that they own all domain names that can be associated with their principal brands.

Arguably even more alarming was the very laid back approach to social media. In several instances the principal brand names were owned by third parties on major social media sites, such as Twitter and YouTube. This is likely to be a consequence of technology moving and evolving more quickly than the management of the brand-owning companies can keep up with.

Some companies, especially the smaller ones, do not view brand risks as a major concern. However, that may be a consequence of either a lack of awareness of the scale of the potential risks or a lack of resource to tackle the issue. A small company is unlikely to hire someone just to manage the brand risk.

There is an argument that outsourcing to a specialist company that can, for example, systematically monitor the Internet and social media is potentially the most cost effective solution to managing the brand risk. This is especially true for smaller companies who do not have the resources to manage this wholly in-house. However, the brand owning company itself is ultimately responsible for protecting what is a very valuable asset or set of assets. Brands have a large intrinsic and financial value attached to them and they need to be defended and protected more assertively than they appear to be at the moment.

To summarise some of the findings from the interviews:

3.4.1 The Practicalities of Brand Risk Management

We have 600 domains. We cannot follow [them all] and it costs a fortune (AudioCom).

We used to have a tool to monitor eBay, but it was overwhelming (AudioCom).

If you could search for everything on the Internet it would be just what we needed, however it must be very expensive (GamblingCom).

We have a lot of local domains, which we do not use anymore. We need to clean up (ChemicalCom).

We cleaned up [the domain portfolio], when I started here. It was too expensive. Now [the portfolio] has grown considerably again (EnergyCom).

Our experience tells us that the volume of diversions is very small. It is not something we can measure. I doubt that it has any major effect (AudioCom).

One of the challenges of online brand risk management is the sheer scale of the task. Many of the interviewees commented on the overwhelming size of the domain catalogues that they had to monitor and maintain. Some of the companies had good housekeeping of these sites and would have a clear out to dispose of domain names that were no longer needed.

Other companies, however, especially the smaller ones, chose to ignore the problem. Their logic was that their products would speak for themselves and that online presence is not necessarily their main mode of advertising. Word of mouth recommendations were cited as being more important in one example. Furthermore, if even the larger companies were struggling to protect all of their brands all of the time with their larger resources, then a smaller company would struggle reach a similar level of protection without unsustainable investment in a brand protection team. Outsourcing the protection is clearly a model of interest here.

Psychologically, it is easier to ignore a potential risk where the risk is not readily quantifiable. However, that is not to say that brand risks are cost-free. Far from it, they can be highly damaging even to small companies. This is why the solution from NightHawk is addressing this idea by showing brand risk managers the potential financial savings for resolving particular brand risks.

3.4.2 Monitoring Brand Risks

We knew which domains we wanted… We do not do any domain monitoring currently, and it should be considered (CloudCom).

We do not have a systematic process [to monitor Google search results]. I do this ad hoc (CloudCom).

It was completely accidental. There was a colleague in another department, who saw the usage of our logo in a folder (EnergyCom).

Some people in our different business units will see a website. Then they send an e-mail to me, "This we don't like," and then we do something about it (ChemicalCom).

We need a system for monitoring (GamblingCom).

Once in a while – every 14 days – I go into Google to check. It's not noted in my calendar (TransportCom).

As discussed earlier, none of the companies interviewed were monitoring online brand risks in a co-ordinated or systematic fashion. Brand infringements were typically discovered accidentally, often by someone close to the market and reporting to the Legal Department in the first instance.

3.4.3 How to Organize Against Brand Risks

It's a good question. It should be with our Marketing Manager, but I'm involved as well… I have to look into it (CloudCom).

There is a concrete evaluation case by case… There is not a general strategy (ChemicalCom).

We still don't have a procedure when we launch a new product. Right now everything is quite accidental (GamblingCom).

Christian said, "Have you registered it?" and I said "You tell me." Until today we both thought that the task was on the other's desk (GamblingCom).

When I stopped at EnergyCom, my co-workers called and said "You are the soul of our brand. Who shall we call now?" (EnergyCom).

At the beginning of my career I reacted to something (user complaints), which I forwarded to my boss. "Should we react to this?" because the complaint was really brutal. He said "No, leave it." (EnergyCom).

> We are too careful (about social media). We don't know what we want…We will protect the brand, however we are very slow (EnergyCom).

> We are not world champions at handling it. We don't own the Twitter handle (CloudCom).

The brand Risk Maps typically identified social media usernames as one of the most important brand risks to consider. This brand risk represented a new threat not seen by companies before. While domain names were a similarly new problem a few years ago, they at least represent a fairly stable problem nowadays. URL naming strategies evolve slowly over time, with the availability of new domain names becoming available being generally well advertised, even in the mainstream media. However, social media presents a rapidly evolving landscape. New services are being created continuously. Keeping track of all the new and existing social media services and monitoring potential brand infringements across this wide range of services is potentially a very major task. This challenge requires companies to be able to develop a robust, yet flexible brand risk management strategy that is distributed across, and embedded in, the whole company. Keeping the activities in separate silos, where collective learning is not supported, is almost certain to result in brand risks either going unnoticed or being managed inadequately.

3.5 Summary

In this chapter, we have examined brand risk management strategies. While theoretical models exist for managing brand risk, the reality for many companies is that such models are not being implemented adequately. Brand risk management, as currently implemented, is largely ad hoc and non-systematic. Where brand risks have been averted or controlled, that success has often been based on good fortune, usually as a result of someone stumbling across something untoward and having the presence of mind to report it to the correct department in the brand-owning company. However, as the social media space continues to grow, such chance discoveries will become less likely and simultaneously the chance of a major brand risk lurking out there undetected increases. Brand owners need to be able to identify, quantify and manage these risks.

One of the elements that is clearly missing in current brand risk management strategies is an effective method of representing the risk threats. It is easy to ignore threats that appear to be abstract and intangible. We would suggest that a method of making the threats more tangible would help focus the minds of brand owners, as they will be able to get a much better view of the scale and proximity of the threats. In the next chapter, we discuss the steps involved in designing and developing a brand risk management process based on the observations and lessons learned from this chapter.

References

1. Abrahams, D.: Brand Risk—Adding Risk Literacy to Brand Management. Gower Publishing, UK (2008)
2. Argyris, C., Schön, D.: Organizational Learning: A Theory of Action Perspective. Addison-Wesley, Reading (1978)
3. Copulsky, J.: Brand Resilience—Managing Risk and Recovery in a High-Speed World. Palgrave Macmillan, Basingstoke (2011)
4. Funston, F., Wagner S., Ristuccia, H.: Ten essential skills for surviving and thriving in uncertainty. Deloitte Review 2010 (2010). http://www.deloitte.com/assets/Dcom-UnitedStates/LocalAssets/Documents/IMOs/GovernanceandRiskManagement/us_grm_RiskIntelligentDecisionMaking.pdf
5. Illeriis, K.: Workplace learning and learning theory. J. Workplace Learn. **15**(4), 167–178 (2003)
6. Kolb, D.: Experiential Learning: Experience as the Source of Learning and Development. Prentice Hall, Englewood Cliffs (1984)
7. Moore, G.: Crossing the Chasm. Capstone Publishing Ltd, Oxford (1991)
8. Schulz, M., Jobe, L.: Codification and Tacitness as Knowledge Management Strategies. An Empirical Exploitation. University of Washington, Seattle (1998)
9. Weber, L.: Sticks and Stones : How Digital Business Reputations are Created Over Time and Lost in a Click. Wiley, Hoboken (2009)

Chapter 4
Designing a Brand Risk Management Process

Abstract Having looked at the nature of brand risk and the levels of awareness and ability to manage risk of a range of brand owners, it is clear that a new approach to brand risk management is required. It is unlikely that a one-size-fits-all approach is likely to work given the scale and variety of the nature of brand risks. Consequently, this chapter focuses on the process by which a brand owning organisation can develop its own custom brand risk management process. Rather than developing the process from traditional brand risk and business theory, a new approach was taken, that of applying the principles of engineering design and interaction design to make a more user-friendly solution. This combined approach relies on developing an understanding of the risks faced by a particular brand owner, the full context of those risks and also the brand owner's capabilities for identifying and managing those risks. Gaining this understanding is facilitated by mapping the risks and the available skills and then synthesising these into tools for designing a new process. An example of how this may be accomplished is the use of personas within defined context scenarios to tell particular brand risk stories. Using those stories, a more complete brand risk management process can be developed.

Keywords Interaction design • Context scenarios • Personas • Awareness • Identification • Assessment • Assignment • Action

4.1 Interaction Design

The notion of "interaction design" came to prominence in the 1970s and 80s with the development of the personal computer. It was clear that there was a barrier between man and machine, and interaction design was the key to breaking down this barrier. Pioneers such as Bill Moggridge and Bill Verplank, who where

C. Hofman and S. Keates, *Countering Brandjacking in the Digital Age*, SpringerBriefs in Computer Science, DOI: 10.1007/978-1-4471-5580-5_4,

working on the first laptop computer (the GRiD Compass), coined the term "interaction design." However it was not until much later that it became more widely adopted.

According to interaction designer Kim Goodwin:

> design is the craft of visualizing concrete solutions that serve human needs and goals within certain constraints [3].

Interaction design focuses on the form and behaviour of interactive products, services and systems. Historically most software companies have had a difficult time developing successful products. According to Bill Buxton [1], it comes down to the fact that the design process is not integrated in the product development.

The classic example is when the engineering team is instructed to deliver a completed project to an extremely tight timescale. Many professional project managers are trained in methodologies, such as Prince 2, which focus on how to manage a process to meet a timetable. However, they almost always lack a full understanding of the role of design in the creation of a new product. Effectively their view of how a product gets developed is shown in the left hand diagram in Fig. 4.1. Consequently, there is no strategic approach to establishing the full set of design requirements. Basically, the users are frozen out of the process, as it becomes purely an exercise in engineering. Any utility or usability offered by the final product is almost exclusively down to chance at this point.

A more complete process is shown in the right hand diagram in Fig. 4.1, where design has been added as an initial activity that aims to provide a better understanding of the product requirements. Activities that would typically be undertaken during this stage would include, for example:

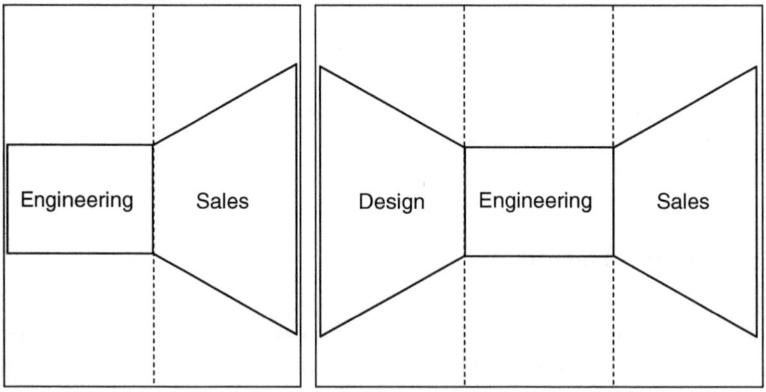

Fig. 4.1 Product development process. The role of design is added in the right hand representation. The wide left hand edge and narrower right hand edge of the Design trapezium reflect the notion that design builds upon the widest possible base of inputs and focuses down towards an, ideally, optimal solution that can than be Engineered into a final product ready for sale to the widest possibly audience. The expansive shape of the Sales trapezium reflects that often products may end up being used for purposes not originally envisaged by the design team [1]

- identification and profiling of target users
- competitive review of existing products
- refinement of the design specification
- creation, evaluation and selection of concept design solutions.

This list is not exhaustive, but serves to illustrate the variety of activities that can be included in design. Different companies obviously place different emphases on each of these activities. More complete descriptions of the role of design in generating products that are genuinely usable and accessible have been discussed by Keates and Clarkson [4, 5].

Even when companies include an explicit design stage in the product development process, this is still no guarantee that the resultant product will be useful or usable. It is not unknown for an initial design team to identify user needs and associated required functionalities, but to then find that it has no, or severely limited, possibility to influence later decisions made during the engineering phase. The process is too rigid in its form. So, while the introduction of design into the process is an improvement on a simple engineering plus sales approach, restricting design solely to an upfront activity limits the potential value of its contribution to the product development process. The consequence of this approach to developing a new product is often project overrun both for cost and for time and a final product that is likely not to live up to user needs and expectations.

Design and engineering are generally considered to be two different processes with different skills and one should not replace the other. In an ideal product development process, "design" and "engineering" activities are wholly complementary and both are present throughout the entire process, albeit with changing levels of prominence. However, many companies do not integrate design across the complete product development process. Buxton [1] argues that companies (think they) know, what they want at the start of the project, and that they know enough to start the project. However ignoring the design phase can cost dearly later if the correct foundations are not in place.

Getting an accurate understanding of the user needs, wants and aspirations is essential for successful product development. Donald Norman has proposed a model, The Seven Stages of Action [6], to identify the user psychology behind every user action. This model is shown in Fig. 4.2.

The model shows the different sequences that the user goes through to complete a goal. Upon completion of any activity or interaction with the product, the user will perceive what happened, interpret the results and evaluate them. The importance of the model lies in the direct connection between the goal, intentions, action and feedback. When they do not correspond, there is something wrong and a re-design is most likely required. Alan Cooper [2] argues that Norman's approach, while correct, is not sufficient to provide a solution that positions a product successfully in the marketplace. It only asks the question "What?" while Cooper is looking to answer the "Why?" He coins the term goal-directed design, which asks, "what are the user goals?" In his opinion, the difference between "tasks" and "goals" is the user motivations.

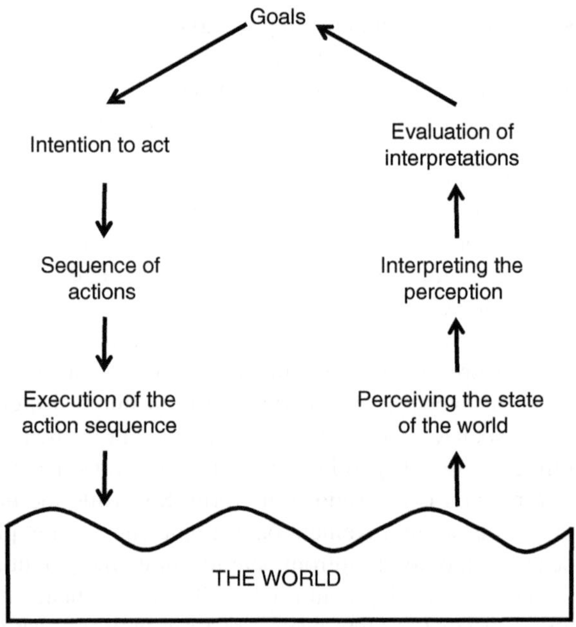

Fig. 4.2 Activity-centred design [6]

While the task considered in this book is to discover and manage brand risks, the user motivations could be to do a good job and to possibly gain promotion when a brand risk is identified and eliminated. On the other hand, the motivation could simply be to avoid being criticized by a line manager when a brand risk is left unresolved. Cooper has outlined a set of principles [2] to serve as guidelines for good design solutions. According to Cooper:

> the single most important process change, we can make is to design our interactive products completely before any programming begins [2].

This is the same viewpoint that Bill Buxton proposes regarding integrating design into the complete product development process:

> Is this up-front process expensive? Absolutely. But it costs nothing compared to the costs that will likely be incurred, if you don't make the investment! [1].

Implicit in much of interaction design theory is an understanding of the task, the context of use and the users. In our case here, the task is the protection of brand reputation and brand value.

The context of use is much more complex, though. It will typically be within a brand owner, which could be a company or corporation, but could also be a public body or a charity. The brand owners could be anything from large multinationals to very small, bespoke manufacturers. They could be selling products, services or systems. They could also have different organisational structures and different levels of complexity and sophistication in how they manage brand risks. However, common to all contexts of use is the need to identify brand risks as quickly as possible and to have a robust, effective and efficient brand risk management system in place.

Complicating the matter further, most brand risks arise from psychological or sociological origins. They are at their most damaging when they affect a person's perception of a brand. If enough people have their perceptions changed by the brand risk, then the consequences for the brand can be fatal, as we have seen in numerous examples earlier in this book (see, for example, the fate of the Ratner jewellery chain).

The fact that brand risks almost invariably include a human component means the detection and evaluation of the level of threat posed by each potential risk will most likely continue to require human input and oversight for the foreseeable future. In other words, any brand risk management process or strategy has to support the people involved in it to ensue that they can identify and manage the risks as effectively and efficiently as possible.

The most common solution for designing for people is to follow user-centred design principles. This, in turn, is usually achieved through participatory design involving activities such as focus groups, interviews, user evaluations and think aloud sessions. The data collected from such sessions can be highly informative, but can also be quite diverse and challenging to summarise. One technique for doing so is the development of personas—i.e. embodiments of user types that can help focus the design process around "people."

4.2 Brand Risk Management Personas

For our purposes here, the user interviews described in Chap. 3 were used to create two personas that represent different aspects of brand risk management. According to Goodwin [3], personas are archetypes that describe the various goals and observed behaviour patterns among potential users. The persona explains the most critical behavioural data in a way that makes it easier to understand how the solution fits. Models such as these are used extensively in design and personas are a powerful tool to better understand users and communicate their wants, needs and aspirations succinctly and in a user-friendly format. It is easier to visualise a "real" person experiencing a real problem and possible solution to that problem than to read through a list of design requirement. Personas make the problem more "human."

Alan Cooper [2] considers personas as better tools than workflow models and physical models, but he warns about incorporating insignificant behaviour patterns, which will only create noise. In other words, it is important to identify the relevant facets of the persona and not cloud the issue with irrelevant ones. Here we will discuss the development of two personas based on the interviews described in Chap. 3. The first step in doing so is to identify the common roles involved in a brand risk management process. Table 4.1 shows these roles.

Table 4.1 The common roles in brand risk management

Table	Expected roles	Description
Brand risk management	Watchdogs	Watchdogs can be anyone in the organization who sees the public face of the brand, usually someone with direct contact to the market/clients
	Administrators	The administrators have the overall responsibility of the service and distribute assignments to task solvers
	Task solvers	Task solvers are qualified according to the type of brand risk

Each of the different roles has example tasks and end goals as shown in Table 4.2.

From these roles, we can create example personas for two of the roles: Administration and Task solver. Watchdogs are arguably too ad hoc across the companies interviewed for a sensible persona to be created.

4.2.1 Persona 1: Brand Risk Administration

Mary Federspiel

Age: 35

Position: Legal Manager

Company: SportsEyez

Based in: Stockholm

Mary finished Law School seven years ago, and after two years as a legal assistant she is now the legal manager at SportsEyez.com. SportsEyez provides European sports data and statistics to players worldwide. Together with a colleague, she handles all the legal areas of the business from contracts, Intellectual Property and infringements of rights. She calculates that she is spending 20–30 % of her time on infringement cases. She regards herself as highly organized and structured, which is a necessity in her position where there is often limited time to deal with a broad spectrum of legal issues. She feels that she plays an important part in the company, and she is highly motivated to shape the future of SportsEyez.

Table 4.2 The common role-specific goals for brand risk management

Roles	Tasks	Role-specific goal
Watchdogs	Observe what happens in the field Filter brand risk information Pass brand risk alerts on to brand risk administration	Be able to detect what is a brand risk and make sure that the information is communicated
Administration	Detect, assign and monitor brand risks	Ensure that brand value is not damaged through brand risks
Task solver	Solve brand risk tasks that are assigned to them	Take appropriate action to resolve the risk

The world is moving and this requires that she stays alert to what is happening in the marketplace and industry. She participates in seminars and networks with other legal practitioners to keep abreast of the latest developments. Her personal network of contacts is both on LinkedIn and via more formal groups outside the Internet. She has close contact with the Marketing and Product Departments, as she is involved when they work on new products or marketing campaigns.

She registers the European trademark with a trademark agency and the domain names via a domain name registrar. Either she registers the domains herself via their control panel or she sends an e-mail to the domain manager there. When the domains are registered, she notifies the Marketing Department, because they have to perform the technical setting up of the domains. Any domain renewal and trademark renewal is taken care of by her or her colleague. She also renews the domain names annually, usually when she receives a renewal reminder from the registrar.

The trademarks are renewed every seven years, when the trademark agency informs her that they are due for renewal. Two years ago, SportsEyez cleaned up their domain name portfolio as they had hundreds of surplus domain names that they did not use. She took the opportunity to recover some domain names that had been taken by cybersquatters. In some cases the domains were handed over without too much difficulty, but she also had a couple of cases that had to be decided at court.

Having seen the drain on resources involved in pursuing the court cases, she has realised that SportsEyez has to be more pro-active in securing and registering their domain names in a timely manner. She uses the calendar in Microsoft Outlook to track the status of where she is in the process of pursuing cybersquatters, such as prompts to send out warning letters to third-party registrants. She uses templates that she developed from earlier experience of such cases. Sometimes she receives an e-mail from a colleague regarding a domain name registered by a third party and she will then see if the company can recover it.

The trademark agency sends Mary a report every time that someone applies for a similar trademark to the one owned by SportsEyez. It is difficult to predict when these notices will be received, since it depends on other parties. It can be every week, month or every second month. Mary will usually dispute these applications. However, these disputes also take time and effort and so in some cases she does not dispute the application when it does not interfere with their trademark class and geographic territory. Every once in a while, when she has the time, Mary performs Google searches to see if anyone else is using their name in domain names or Google Adwords. However, her search strategy is ad hoc, using random search terms, as she does not have the technical knowledge to structure a systematic strategy. The variety of possibilities for brand infringements is simply too great for her to manage on her own. She is not aware of all of the different forms of social media or the registrations processes, nor does she have the time to keep fully up to date on all the latest trends in the technology.

She did receive an offer from a monitoring service, but it seemed expensive and she feels that it would just mean a lot more work, as there would be yet another relationship for her to manage. She is sometimes informed about infringements by business partners or someone else in SportsEyez, who may have seen something strange or been told about something suspicious by a client. They typically inform her by e-mail when they come across such instances. However, she does not know whether everyone in the company knows to contact her when they find such a problem. Consequently, she cannot be sure that she is informed every time someone within the company finds such a potential infringement, so she has no idea how many other infringements are going unreported.

Mary meets formally with the Sales and Marketing Departments every six months to discuss relevant issues and to share each other's experiences. She feels that the Marketing Department underestimates the scale of brand risk and the need for brand protection. She feels that one of the best defences is that product names should be unique and not generic, as they are more defensible.

4.2.2 Persona 2: Task Solver

John Goldsmith
Age: 39
Position: Online Marketing Manager
Company: SportsEyez
Based in: Stockholm

John has a Bachelors degree in Marketing from his local Business School. Before joining SportsEyez, he worked as the Nordic Area Sales Manager for four years at a rival company. He enjoys his work in a fast-paced environment where he feels that he makes a difference. He is part of the five man Sales and Marketing team, which promotes the SportsEyez brand worldwide. He is mainly responsible for the online marketing at SportsEyez. He manages a web designer, a programmer and an intern, who help oversee traffic statistics, keep their Facebook page updated and send out Twitter messages. His typical day consists of meetings, answering e-mails and preparing new campaigns. He uses his PC for most of his work, however he is away from his desk a lot of the time where his smartphone comes in handy to check e-mails. He has recently found some apps that have helped him with some work-related tasks. He is currently doing an MBA on the side, making his life rather stressful, but he tries to balance his commitments.

John is in regular contact with the Legal Department, especially when they plan to launch new products and also, because they are a small company with only 50 or so employees, almost everyone knows everyone else. He feels that the Legal Department is very cautious, while he just wants to go ahead and take action. Brand risk is not really an area he is involved or interested in. However Mary from the Legal Department did once tell him to register their brand on Twitter during a business lunch, so he did. He has experienced a situation where the domain name that he wanted for a marketing campaign had been taken by someone else. He e-mailed Mary to see if they could get it, because obviously they had the rights to the domain. However, in his opinion, no harm was done to the SportsEyez brand. He will find another domain name if this one is not recovered.

4.3 Design Considerations

As the personas have been created, we will now set up the vision for the design of a brand risk management process and the design requirements to enable the identified personas to be able to accomplish their goals.

Building on the initial problem, we now understand the personas, their targets and their goals. The vision statement can be built directly from the user needs. This leads to the following problem and vision statements:

4.3.1 Problem Statement

Due to not having a suitable brand risk management process to confront widespread brand infringements, brand owners may suffer lost identity, counterfeiting, the spreading of false rumours and sales channel conflicts on the Internet. These risks have direct and indirect negative outcomes, such as lost turnover to competitors, counterfeiters and sales partners and general damage to the brand resulting in loss of brand status, reputation and value.

4.3.2 The Vision Statement

To create a process that empowers brand owners to understand, detect early and successfully manage or eliminate brand risk.

Taking these statements as the guiding principles, we can begin to build a risk management process. The next stage is to identify all of the relevant aspects to be addressed.

A brainstorming session can be used to identify the different elements included in a brand risk management process. Such sessions can take many forms, but an effective approach is to share ideas via post-it notes or white boards, where participants can contribute ideas freely. Those notes can then be clustered. Such a session for a brand risk management process identified six clusters of importance: Awareness, Identification, Assessment, Assignment, Action and The Unknown, which are described below.

4.3.3 Awareness: What do We Know About Brand Risks?

The first step in introducing any new process is to establish the level of knowledge that exists. Does the organisation have a view on what brand risk is and where it may come from? How many people know what a brand risk is? How many of them know what to do if they encounter a brand infringement, such as a cybersquatter or counterfeiter? A comprehensive audit of knowledge and awareness is required so that existing processes can either be strengthened or replaced with more effective solutions.

4.3.4 Identification: How are Brand Risks Identified?

No brand risk management process will work without education and awareness of the risks throughout the organisation. Many brand infringements are identified by chance: someone stumbles across something that does not quite look right and reports it. Making everyone in the organisation aware of brand infringements and brand risks makes the entire workforce into eyes and ears on the lookout for such risks. Once a risk has been identified, it is important that this information is communicated swiftly and effectively to the correct people.

Risks come in different forms and early identification of risks is one of the most important factors in controlling and managing them successfully. Many brand owners rely on ad hoc methods of identifying risks, such as members of staff doing non-systematic searches on Google or relying on chance discoveries, such as stumbling across a cybersquatter following a typographical error in a URL. The most effective brand risk management tactic is to identify potential risks before they can become extant risks. Prevention is undoubtedly better than cure here. To be able to do this, though, requires brand owners to take a proactive stance in trying to find out where new risks and opportunities for brand promotion may arise, such as the advent of new technologies or social media outlets.

4.3.5 Assessment: How Great is the Risk?

For any risk management process to be effective, the scale of the threat posed by the risk needs to be quantified. The potential for a risk to do significant harm to a brand is a combination of three factors:

- the magnitude or size of the harm that can be done
- the probability of the risk actually generating harm
- the proximity of the threat, i.e. how soon it may happen.

Another useful indicator is the trending or direction of the threat, i.e. whether these factors are increasing or decreasing over time. Standard methods and practices are available for estimating each of these factors from the discipline of risk analysis. The ultimate purpose of the assessment activities is to provide a prioritised list of potential brand risks so that the brand owner can focus efforts on those risks that are considered the most serious, that is those with the most damaging combination of magnitude, probability and proximity.

4.3.6 Assignment: Who does What?

A brand risk management process needs to be supported by appropriate internal structures, with clear lines of communication and responsibilities. The management process is likely to involve several departments within an organisation and so proactive effort is required to ensure that the flow of information between those departments happens effectively and that everyone knows their roles and responsibilities. The system should also be designed to be robust to changes in technology and also changes in personnel. Brand owners must be aware of the risks of leaving the majority of brand protection in the hands of a very limited number of individuals. There is a temptation to make one person solely responsible for brand risk management and if that person leaves, then the knowledge will depart with them. One method for militating against this risk is to ensure that all processes are written down and comprehensive records of all decisions and actions are kept.

4.3.7 Action: How do We Manage this?

As we have put forward elsewhere in this book, prevention is the best method for managing brand risks. However, even the best prevention is not always completely watertight and some risks will always make it through.

Not all brand risks require a response, though. In many cases, the brand owners may decide that the cost of managing a risk exceeds the potential damage that may arise from the risk. For example, if a competitor defames their brand, then that may well justify a response. However, if a lone blogger with a minimal number of followers does the same, then that is most likely not worth the time and effort to correct. So, the first action that is required is judgement—is this risk worth pursuing and managing?

Should a risk be considered sufficiently serious, then the actions available to the brand owner will be contingent upon the nature of the risk. Most risks can be managed through legal avenues, such as closing down counterfeit sites, retrieving cybersquatter sites and serving "cease and desist" notices on defamers. However, recourse to legal actions is almost always very expensive and not always guaranteed to resolve the issue. Some brand owners prefer to resolve some threats by opening their chequebooks and buying off the risk. In some instances this will be cheaper and less risky than going to court. However, it has the typical disadvantage of all "ransom" approaches, in that it may actively encourage others to present themselves as brand risks in the hope of financial gain.

Brand owners should make themselves aware of all of the possible methods and tools available for managing brand risks.

4.3.8 Preparedness: What do We not Know? How do We Handle this?

Brand risks, especially in the ever-changing social media space, are constantly evolving. New technologies mean new opportunities and new threats—the two go hand in hand. Once brand owners have a brand risk management process in place, they should not assume that is their job done. All processes of this type need reflective evaluations and updating regularly, especially when deficiencies are identified. Brand owners need to ask questions such as:

- Are we identifying all of the brand risks?
- Are we dealing with them efficiently and effectively?
- Are we satisfied with our process?
- Are we keeping abreast of all relevant new technologies and risks?
- Do any of our processes, tools, skills or knowledge need updating or improving?

Having identified the overall shape and contents of a brand risk management process, the next step is to begin to personalise it to a human level, so that the different actors can understand how such a process relates to them.

In the case of the two personas developed here, they have similar expectations. They expect a process that clearly identifies information flows, tasks, roles and responsibilities.

In Mary's case, she would like to have the identified brand risks arrive on her desk and for her to be able to trust that all of the major risks had been identified and ideally each with its own quantified risk assessment. She would then review the available courses of action for each risk. Where the course of action was wholly within her remit, she would then act on it, sending out the necessary warning letters or beginning legal proceedings. She would expect to be able to produce summary reports periodically to inform the brand risk champion within the company.

John would like to be able to use the brand risk management process to proactively identify potential risks, so that he could take defensive decisions to reduce the potential for risk. For example, if there were two possible brand names that he was considering, he would like to be able to make a comparison of the defensibility of both as part of his overall judgement for which name to use. This would include whether third parties had already taken the relevant social media names or Internet domains.

Having established the personas and their expectations, we can begin to elaborate examples of how the personas may operate within a brand risk management process. To assist with this, we can use context scenarios. A context scenario should focus on a persona's activities, motivations and mental model of what is happening and what needs to be done. It should show the touch points that the user has with the brand risk management process during a specific period to achieve certain desired outcomes. Scenarios should avoid going into technical details and focus mainly on the big picture.

4.4 Context Scenarios for Brand Risk Management

To illustrate possible context scenarios for a brand risk management process, we present two examples for SportsEyez in which Mary needs to manage two brand risks. These context scenarios were verified through discussions with representatives from CloudCom and GamblingCom.

In this case, it is assumed that an online brand risk management application has been developed to automate as many of the standard processes as possible. That application is accessed via a login page and controlled via a dashboard. An external brand risk monitoring agency has been hired by SportsEyez as specialists in identifying potential brand risks. That company has developed and hosts the brand risk management application that SportsEyez uses.

Context scenario 1 for Mary Federspiel:

1. Mary arrives as always at 08:30 in the morning at the office. The first thing she does on arrival is to check her e-mail on her computer. She scans quickly to see if there are any urgent issues that require her immediate attention. The remaining e-mails she handles later in the day, depending on her schedule. She usually has one hour set aside for this before any other scheduled tasks or meetings.
2. She finds that she has received an e-mail from the external brand risk monitoring agency that she hired two months earlier. That e-mail informs her that two new brand risks have been identified. First, SportsEyez still has not registered a new brand name that they launched last month as a YouTube username. Second, a domain name that could be diverting SportsEyez customers has been flagged up and is owned by a known cybersquatter. Given the significant volume of traffic that the domain generates, it should be recovered as quickly as possible.
3. Mary clicks on the link in the e-mail to arrive at the brand risk management agency's login page. She logs in and arrives at the dashboard page. She can see the two new brand risks. Given that YouTube and other social media is Marketing's area, she forwards the task to John Goldsmith, the Online Marketing manager.
4. She turns her attention to the other task, which is the cybersquatter's domain name. A brief description gives her the information needed to understand the situation. She can see that this is a valuable domain name and selects one of the choices given to her by the system to retrieve the domain name. The system confirms that she will get a reminder if there has been no reply from the cybersquatter within, say, 14 days.
5. She logs out of the application, because she has a meeting at 10:00.
6. After the meeting and lunch, she looks in her e-mail inbox and there is an e-mail from the external agency. It confirms the action taken earlier and there is also a message from John confirming the brand risk notification.
7. Three days later, when she opens her inbox in the morning there is an e-mail from the external agency informing her that there has been no reply from the cybersquatter. She logs in again to the agency's application via the link in the e-mail and upgrades the status to send a "cease and desist" letter. She can see in the Status section of the system that John has updated his task to Completed.

Context scenario 1 for John Goldsmith:

1. John arrives to the office at 08:45. Today he has a meeting with a developer at 09:15, so he has time to get a cup of coffee from the coffee machine. On his way down to the kitchen, he checks his e-mails on his mobile.
2. He sees that he has an e-mail from Mary regarding an urgent issue. While sipping his coffee, he reads the e-mail, which explains about the situation regarding YouTube and why it is recommended that SportsEyez registers the name. He does not really have time now and will look at it later.
3. After the meeting with the developer, he is at his desk going through his e-mails. It is just one of those busy mornings and he is also scheduled to meet with Sales before lunch. On his computer, he sees the e-mail from earlier about YouTube. He clicks on the link in the e-mail, logs into the system and accesses the user dashboard.
4. On the dashboard, he finds the brand risk description explaining why they should register the user name and also the step-by-step instructions for doing so. The system tells him that it takes an estimated five minutes to get the name, so he has just enough time to do it before his next meeting. Once done, he updates the status of the task to Completed and logs out of the system.
5. Sitting on the train on his way home from work, he remembers about another e-mail from Mary. He checks his mobile and finds it. The e-mail was a reminder about some domain names that she recommends he register to protect the new brand they have just released. He clicks the link on the e-mail and logs into the system again. There is an option to assign this task to the external domain registrar company that they use, which he accepts. He logs out just before the train reaches his stop.
6. The next morning on the train he checks his mobile. There is a confirmation from the registrar company that the domains he ordered the previous day have been registered. He archives the e-mail and leans back into the seat to enjoy the rest of the journey.

Context scenario 2 for Mary Federspiel:

1. Mary and John meet Bo from Sales for their quarterly meeting to share the latest news and follow up on issues regarding trademarks and other legal updates of interest.
2. Mary wants to get the team to think more proactively about brand risk and so she has commissioned a report from the external brand risk agency, showing the brand risks for the last quarter. Mary presents an overall status, where the other team members can see the brand risk tasks solved in the last quarter and the results that have been achieved. She thanks the other members for helping out and would like their input to improve the brand risk management processes further.
3. Bo asks why this is really necessary. "*Why all the to-do just to get back a couple of domain names?*" Mary shows him that there are many types of brand risks other than solely domain names. "*Bo, did you know that last month the*

system discovered a case of digital piracy. Someone had sent out a copy of our latest report? The one we sell for US$1,000 per unit. It could undermine our whole business. There is no way we could detect this and stop it in time without a more comprehensive and systematic plan." She shows a visual model explaining savings made. She adds that the company could actually avoid brand risks by being more proactive in the first place, when new brands are launched or marketing campaigns are being created.

4. John from Marketing explains that he registered their YouTube channel some time ago and that it is a welcome development that they are being more proactive in this area. However, he needs to understand better what it purpose it serves. Perhaps they will never use YouTube for marketing purposes and at that time they will just use another name, if the one that they want is not available.
5. Mary turns to the Social Media section in her report. "*John, did you know that YouTube appears in Google search results, and it's a great way to get traffic? I mean, even if we don't use it then at least it is blocked for anyone else. We pay several thousand dollars for our trademarks, so we have an obligation to protect them on the Internet.*"
6. One of the other team members saw recently that someone had copied some of their sports stats and put them on their website. "*We do have a challenge with these types of piracy. Mary, will you be able to investigate these types of cases as well and stop them?*" Mary leans back in the chair. "*It is possible to investigate these as well. We can add this to our brand risk management process.*"
7. After the meeting, Mary returns to her office and begins to sketch out possible revisions to the brand risk management process. She recognises that internal communication about the need to manage brand risk is required, as it is clear that not everyone sees the benefits of this. She also decides to schedule regular meetings with the technology teams to keep up to date on the latest trends in social media. Finally, she sets up a call with the external agency to thank them for the report and commission a similar one for the current quarter.

4.5 Summary

This chapter has highlighted the steps that a brand owner can follow to construct a brand risk management process. We have examined the need for a design process to provide a structure to the development of a brand risk management process and given example problems and vision statements that provide an intellectual drive behind the creation of the process. In conjunction with brand risk management experts, we have highlighted six areas of knowledge that need to be addressed. Example personas were created based on the interviews with brand risk owners presented in Chap. 3 and example context scenarios also discussed.

In the next chapter, we will review what we have learned about brand risk management.

References

1. Buxton, B.: Sketching User Experiences—Getting the Design Right and the Right Design. Morgan Kaufmann Publishers, San Francisco (2007)
2. Cooper, A.: About Face 3: The Essentials of Interaction Design. John Wiley and Sons, New York (2007)
3. Goodwin, K.: Designing for the Digital Age. Wiley Publishing Inc, Indianapolis (2009)
4. Keates, S., Clarkson, P.J.: Countering Design Exclusion: An Introduction to Inclusive Design. Springer, London (2003)
5. Keates, S.: Designing for Accessibility: A Business Guide to Countering Design Exclusion. Lawrence Erlbaum Associates, Mahwah (2006)
6. Norman, D.: The Psychology of Everyday Things. Basic Books, New York (1988)

Chapter 5
Brand Risks in Cyberspace

Abstract One of the difficulties in writing a book like this is knowing when to stop writing. Through the course of writing this one, we have been paying attention to the stream of stories in mainstream media arising from brandjacking, cybersquatting and an assorted collection of other dubious or suspect practices in cyberspace. The consequences of these examples are almost always financial or reputational damage, either for the brand owner or for the infringing party. This concluding chapter explores some of the more recent stories of brand risk in the news, to show how brand risks are here to stay and are continuously evolving as new technologies become available. The chapter finishes by reviewing the overall content of the book to summarise the important points we have discussed and explored.

Keywords Facebook • Twitter • Blog • Hacking • Fake reviews • Passwords • Monitoring risks • Managing risks

5.1 Recent Brand Risks in the News

We will examine five examples of brand risks reported in the news during the process of writing this book.

5.1.1 Facebook Misdirection

One example of possible suspect practice involves a Facebook page set up following the murder of an off-duty soldier in Woolwich, London in May 2013. A blogger for a national newspaper has alleged that the page in question, *RIP Woolwich Soldier*, appears to be a front for the English Defence League (EDL), a far-right organisation on the extreme fringes of British political life [5]. The page has been

C. Hofman and S. Keates, *Countering Brandjacking in the Digital Age*,
SpringerBriefs in Computer Science, DOI: 10.1007/978-1-4471-5580-5_5,

"liked" over by over 1 million visitors. Those 1 million visitors have consequently opened up their Facebook timelines to messages posted from an organisation that many of them would most likely have no wish to be associated with (based on the very small membership boasted by the EDL). It is not clear at the time of writing whether the allegation is justified or not, but if it is correct, then this leaves 1 million people exposed to a personal reputational risk, should extreme political messages begin appearing in their personal timelines.

5.1.2 Twitter Libel

Another example is the case of Lord McAlpine versus Sally Bercow. In 2012, the BBC broke a news story alleging a senior conservative politician had been involved in a child sex abuse scandal centred around the Bryn Estyn Children's Home in the 70 and 80s. Two days later Ms. Bercow, the wife of the Speaker of the House of Commons, posted a Twitter entry which read, "*Why is Lord McAlpine trending? *Innocent face**" on 4 November 2012. Lord McAlpine had been the conservative party treasurer during the period that the alleged abuse had taken place. The allegations were subsequently shown to be wholly false and that Lord McAlpine had never even been to the home in question.

However, Ms. Bercow's tweet had been widely reported and Lord McAlpine believed that the tweet was libellous. He pursued the issue through the courts. The High Court judgement made it clear in its opinion that although Ms. Bercow's tweet did not connect the Lord McAlpine explicitly to the alleged abuse, when taken in the wider context of the news story and his personal background, the implication was considered sufficiently defamatory to constitute libel [4]. It is estimated that tweet will end up costing Mrs. Bercow approximately US$100,000 in fees and damages.

5.1.3 Blog Defamation

A similar result was seen in the case of former "Oxo Mum" (so-called from her role as the mother in a famous series of television advertisements for Oxo) Linda Bellingham versus Darren Richards. Ms. Bellingham was co-owner of a real estate business, Virtual Property World. Mr. Richards had written a number of blogs alleging that Ms. Bellingham's husband and business partner had been involved in property fraud. They were alerted to the blogs by the British Franchise Association and they subsequently applied to the high court for an unmasking order, obliging Google and Wordpress to release the IP address of the computer from which the blog entries had originated. The blog entries were traced back to Darren Richards, owner of a rival real estate business. The high court found that the blog entries had been defamatory and Mr. Richards was ordered to pay in excess of US$150,000 in damages, plus legal fees [1].

Although in both of these cases, the defamed parties were successful in their legal actions, going to court can be a traumatic experience and one that is best avoided. It is not clear in either of these cases whether the damages would cover the legal costs incurred in bringing the actions or whether costs were awarded. Fortunately both sets of claimants were individually wealthy enough to proceed with the litigation, but this is not always the case. It is clear, though, that given the willingness of some people to do damage to the good name of others, all brand owners need to have good defences in place against such malicious attacks.

While both defendants subsequently apologised for the distress they had caused those they had defamed, their original allegations can still be found on the Internet. The golden rule is to treat everything posted on the Internet as being permanent and highly public. There is no such thing as total privacy in cyberspace. Ill-considered Internet content can do lasting damage to reputations, so strong "message" control is required if you wish to project a constant and consistent message about a brand and its values.

5.1.4 Twitter Hacking

Another prominent example came from the US, where the Associated Press Twitter account was hacked and hoax messages about bomb explosions at the White House sent markets tumbling until the hoax was discovered. The S&P 500 index had US$136.5 billion of value wiped out in the time taken to correct the misinformation [3]. In today's increasingly automated world, it is vitally important that the correct information is made available. It is also crucial that brand owners secure their networks against such attacks. Although the principal victim of this hoax was the Standard and Poor 500 Index and the companies listed there, the reputation of Associated Press has also been damaged for being the vehicle by which the chaos was allowed to happen.

5.1.5 Fake Reviews

Sometimes companies and organisations can bring bad publicity to their own doors, as a result of misguided attempts to manipulate social media and Internet content unfairly. For example, hotel reviews have long been the subject of debate over which reviews are genuinely from travellers and which ones are not. It has been suspected that unscrupulous rivals may leave strongly negative anonymous comments about their local competition. However, it has also been suspected that sometimes hotels post overly positive reviews about their own property. This was certainly the case for Frank Long, who runs the Ramada Glasgow Airport Hotel. He was found to have e-mailed members of his staff instructing them to leave positive messages on the trip advisor hotel review site following a string of negative reviews. It appears that Mr. Long was aware of the danger of planted reviews being easy to recognise, so he even went as far as providing guidance on how to write a positive, but not overly effusive, review.

His careful preparations became undone when the e-mail was obtained by a reporter for the Daily Record newspaper and subsequently published, representing something of a reputational own goal for Mr. Long and his hotel [6] and a useful warning for others who attempt to manipulate notionally unbiased reviews in this way.

5.2 Summary

In this book we have examined the threats posed by brand risks originating from the Internet and from social media, in particular. In Chap. 1, we explored what risks are and found that risks can come in many different formats, with different levels of severity. We examined how the urgency to address a particular risk is a combination of both its severity and its proximity, i.e. how soon the risk is likely to start having an impact on the brand and its reputation. It is worth remembering, though, that in all cases, the faster that a brand owner can respond to a potential risk, the more contained that risk will usually be. As the old adage goes, a stitch in time saves nine.

Chapter 2 examined these issues in more depth, exploring the concept of what makes a brand a brand and what defines its intrinsic value. The point was made that brands now make up a significant portion of the value of the companies that own them. As such, protecting a brand is, by direct extension, protecting the company itself. Consequently, it makes clear business sense to put in place a strategy for the protection of all of the major brands owned by a company. We suggested that a brand risk management process is required to accomplish this.

Chapter 3 explored the demand for brand risk management and asked the question, "who needs to implement a brand risk management process?" The answer to that question is all brand owners who wish to protect the investment and intrinsic value that their brand represents. However, as can be seen from the interviews with different types of brand owners, not all brand owners are fully aware of the dangers of brand risk. Even if they are aware, they are not necessarily willing or able to address the issue directly. There is a sense that the problem can be too large and too complex to ever really get fully on top of it.

In many regards, this is no different to the attitudes of many companies and individuals towards computer security. It is possible to be lulled into a false sense of security by thinking that there are many, many users out there in cyberspace. Why would anyone want to target *me* when there are much bigger and juicier fish to fry out there? This is why passwords such as "password," "letmein" or "qwerty" continue to be used, despite all the literature warning of the dangers of doing so [2]. Hackers now attack computers on an industrial scale. The power of modern computing makes it easy for them to do so. So, while there may be lots of other people to hide among or behind, the hackers can attack lots of people in one go. The mathematics makes it clear that an inadequately protected computer will be compromised very, very quickly—typically less than 20 min after first connecting the to Internet, if its firewall is not switched on.

Just as hacking has become an industrial-scale activity, it is highly likely that activities such as brandjacking will follow a similar path. There is money to be made by exploiting the time delay between advances in what the technology allows and an organisation's response to those advances. For someone who is dedicated to such malicious practices, that time delay offers a valuable and potentially lucrative window of opportunity. The best defence for a brand owner is to keep that window as small as possible. To do so requires an active policy of keeping abreast of the relevant advances in technology and being able to formulate an effective response quickly. For some companies, this will require more resources and technical knowledge than they might possess. Under those circumstances, the most effective solution may be to contract in a specialist agency to provide the necessary expertise.

Irrespective of who does the monitoring of risks, etc., companies and organisations still need to have a brand risk management process in place. Chapter 4 describes the steps that a brand owner should consider going through to develop such a process. We have not proposed a single model for all circumstances, because such a model would be inherently complex and most likely out-dated quite quickly by new technologies. Instead, we have taken the approach of suggesting a design process that is far more technology—and organisation-agnostic.

For example, not all companies and organisations will have the same internal structure and departments. Responsibilities may be allocated differently. Consequently, a single one-size-fits-all approach to brand risk management process would most likely not work. However, by focusing on the people who could be involved in the process and who should have ownership of it and the contexts in which they may encounter and address brand risks, then a brand owning organisation can identify the brand risk management process best suited to its needs.

Having said that, there are some common messages that can be found. For example, clear lines of communication and responsibility are essential. Everyone must know what they are doing and why. Also, brand risk management is something the whole organisation should engage with. If anyone finds a potential brand risk, they should know who to report it to. Finally, like all new processes, brand risk management works best if there is an organisational champion—someone at the very top who takes a strong leadership role in saying that this is an activity that this organisation takes seriously.

References

1. Brady, T.: Oxo Mum wins high court battle over businessman who attacked her property business. Daily Mail. http://www.dailymail.co.uk/news/article-2312495/Oxo-Mum-Linda-Bellingham-wins-High-Court-battle-businessman-Darren-Richards.html (2013). Accessed 13 Oct 2013

2. Goessl, L.: List of most common passwords released, password still on top. Digital Journal. http://digitaljournal.com/article/335497 (2012). Accessed 25 Oct 2012
3. Selyukh, A.: Hackers send fake market-moving AP tweet on white house explosions. Reuters. http://uk.reuters.com/article/2013/04/23/net-us-usa-whitehouse-ap-idUSBRE93M12Y20130423 (2013). Accessed 13 Oct 2013
4. Shirbon, E.: Ironical tweet was defamatory, context was key, court rules. Reuters. http://uk.reuters.com/article/2013/05/24/uk-britain-twitter-defamation-idUKBRE94N0H020130524 (2013). Accessed 13 Oct 2013
5. Simons, J.W.: RIP woolwich soldier: over a million people may have accidentally liked a covert EDL Facebook page. Daily Telegraph. http://blogs.telegraph.co.uk/news/jakewallissimons/100218409/over-a-million-people-may-have-accidentally-liked-an-edl-facebook-page/ (2013). Accessed 13 Oct 2013
6. Taylor, D.:Ramada boss who ordered false Trip advisor reviews dodges hotel after being exposed. Daily Record. http://www.dailyrecord.co.uk/news/scottish-news/ramada-false-review-boss-dodges-1372096 (2012). Accessed 13 Oct 2012

Appendix 1: Norwegian Air Shuttle Calculation

Question: What happens when you do not own a trademark or have a generic brand name?

Answer: It can cost you a substantial amount of money.

Norwegian Air Shuttle, the airline company commonly referred to simply as "Norwegian," does not have a trademark registration for "Norwegian," because it is too generic. As a consequence, according to our calculations, Norwegian pays an excess surcharge of up to US$1.4 million per year. When you do an Internet search for "Norwegian," the flight company, then the advertisements appearing at the top of the page are bidding to be the top ranked answers for this particular keyword. Figure 1 shows the results for such a search on *google.dk* in May 2013.

Companies bid different amounts over time to compete to be in those first three results. Shortly before Fig. 1 was taken, SAS, one of Norwegian's major competitors in the Scandinavian market, was ranking highly for this search term. It is clearly in Norwegian's interests to ensure that it ranks higher in the search results than SAS does.

If we look at the top three sponsored results in Fig. 1, they are all sales intermediaries, in other words sites that sell flights from many carriers. Two of these sites, *ticket.dk* and *travellink.dk* do at least point to Norwegian specific searches, but *flybillet.dk* does not. That link points to a generic flight search page.

How much extra does it cost Norwegian to allow other bidders for this keyword? Table 1 shows the traffic estimates from Denmark only, using the Google keyword search tool for Norwegian and related searches.

Google estimates that there are approximately 250,000 searches monthly. According to their traffic estimator the average click price for the number one position is US$4. If Norwegian were the only ones to advertise, then the click price could be as low as US$0.10. From other cases it is known that positions one and two, i.e. the top two returned positions, account for 80 % of the Adwords

C. Hofman and S. Keates, *Countering Brandjacking in the Digital Age*,
SpringerBriefs in Computer Science, DOI: 10.1007/978-1-4471-5580-5,

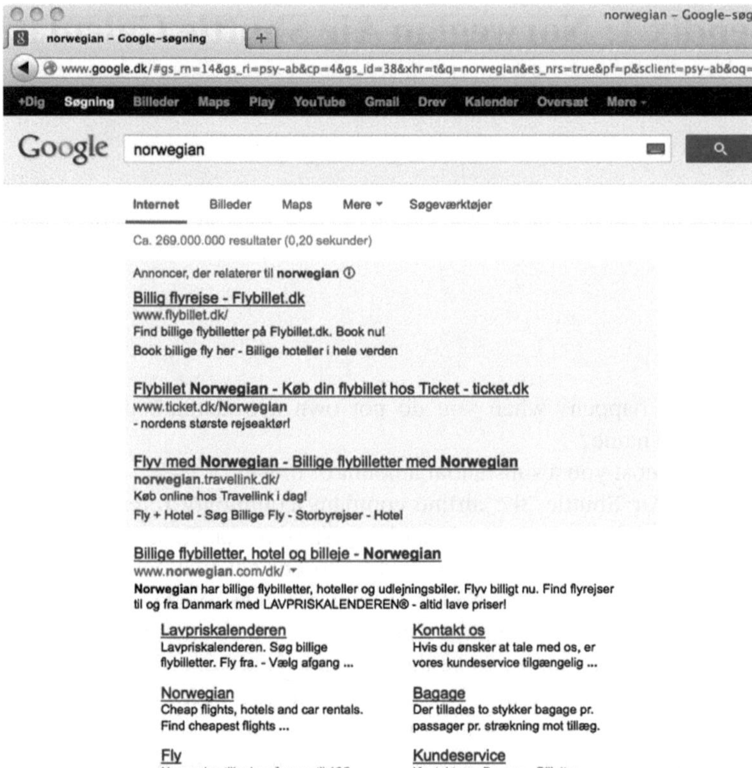

Fig. A. 1 The search results for "Norwegian" on *google.dk*. The results in the *shaded box* at the *top* of the page are returns that companies have bid for to get a high profile position in the results for that search term

Table A. 1 The estimated traffic from Danish searches for the search terms shown

Search term	Estimated traffic
Norwegian	201,000
Norwegian air	27,100
Norwegian airways	5,400
Norwegian airlines	6,600
Norwegian airline	5,400
Total	245,500

traffic, and Adwords is usually 20–30 % of the total traffic. Consequently, the extra cost that Norwegian pays for their Adwords per year is:

250,000 × 30 % × 12 = 900,000 clicks on advertisements including the Norwegian search term 900,000 × 40 % = 360,000 clicks on position 1

$$360,000 \times (4 - 0.10) = \text{US\$}1,404,000 \text{ in surcharges per year} \tag{A.1}$$

From this calculation, it can be estimated that Norwegian is paying US$1.4 million extra because intermediaries and competitors are allowed to compete for their branded search terms. If they had chosen a less generic brand name, then they would be in a better position to protect themselves from such competition.

MIX
Papier aus verantwortungsvollen Quellen
Paper from responsible sources
FSC® C105338

If you have any concerns about our products,
you can contact us on
ProductSafety@springernature.com

In case Publisher is established outside the EU,
the EU authorized representative is:
Springer Nature Customer Service Center GmbH
Europaplatz 3, 69115 Heidelberg, Germany

Printed by Libri Plureos GmbH
in Hamburg, Germany